WILLIAM LANGLAND

PIERS PLOWMAN: THE Z VERSION

edited by A. G. Rigg and Charlotte Brewer

According to the scholarship of the last hundred years, *Piers Plowman* survives in three versions, the **A**, **B**, and **C** texts. This edition presents what the editors believe to be a copy of a version written *before* the **A**-text. The **Z**-version is preserved uniquely in MS Bodley 851, dated before 1388, probably in the 1370s. It is shorter than the **A**-text: many passages (such as the Seven Deadly Sins) are in embryo form, and in the progress from **Z** to **A** to **B** to **C** one can see the poet's imagination at work. **Z** also contains many lines and passages not in the **A** text: some are flat and insipid, while others, though of considerable poetic merit, were rejected in the **A** text for other reasons.

The text is presented with a running concordance with **A**; the use of bold type and typographical symbols enables the reader to recognize **Z**'s peculiarities easily; a concordance table is also provided. The Introduction presents the hypothesis of **Z**'s priority in detail, with an account of the relationship of **Z** to **A**, and of **Z** to the other versions of the poem and to individual manuscripts of the **A** tradition. The commentary discusses points of difficulty and interpretation, and indicates variations from **A**. An appendix describes the language of the **Z** text, and argues that it is linguistically coherent, characteristically West Midland, and shows no signs of being a scribal construct.

The early nature of the **Z**-version is a hypothesis, but, if it is accepted, this edition provides a new tool for assessing not only the textual traditions of the **A**, **B**, and **C** texts but also Langland's development as a poet.

STUDIES AND TEXTS 59

WILLIAM LANGLAND

PIERS PLOWMAN: THE Z VERSION

EDITED BY

A. G. RIGG

AND

CHARLOTTE BREWER

PONTIFICAL INSTITUTE OF MEDIAEVAL STUDIES

ACKNOWLEDGMENT

This book has been published with the help of
a grant from the Canadian Federation for the
Humanities, using funds provided by the
Social Sciences and Humanities Research Council
of Canada.

CANADIAN CATALOGUING IN PUBLICATION DATA

Langland, William, 1330?-1400?
  [Piers the Plowman]
  Piers Plowman: the Z version

(Studies and texts, ISSN 0082-5328 ; 59)
Text in Middle English and Latin, introduction and notes in English.
Includes bibliographical references.
ISBN 0-88844-059-6

I. Rigg, A. G., 1937-   II. Brewer, Charlotte, 1956-   III. Pontifical Institute
of Mediaeval Studies.   IV. Title.   V. Title: Piers the Plowman.   VI. Series:
Studies and texts (Pontifical Institute of Mediaeval Studies) ; 59.

PR2010.R54   821'.1   C82-094882-9

Pontifical Institute of Mediaeval Studies
59 Queen's Park Crescent East
Toronto, Ontario, Canada M5S 2C4

PRINTED BY UNIVERSA, WETTEREN, BELGIUM

To Norman Davis

Contents

PIERS PLOWMAN: THE Z VERSION

Preface

We are aware that the proposition presented here is controversial and in conflict with traditional views of the genesis of *Piers Plowman* and its textual transmission. Nevertheless, we feel that our hypothesis can be tested only by an examination of the text as a whole, and we are therefore pleased to have the opportunity to present the **Z**-text for scholarly scrutiny and debate. The text is printed by permission of the Keeper of Western Manuscripts, Bodleian Library, Oxford.

Our ability to make such a hypothesis rests on the work of others, especially the monumental editions of Kane (the **A**-text) and Kane-Donaldson (the **B**-text), whose meticulous presentation of variant readings has enabled us to proceed with some confidence. Although we recognize that our hypothesis may well be unacceptable – may indeed seem absurd – to previous editors of the poem, we still wish to acknowledge our indebtedness to their fundamental studies.

We have also benefitted from the constructive criticism and encouragement of our colleagues in Toronto (particularly Professors L. E. Boyle, Angus Cameron, and Colin Chase, and Dr. Anne Quick), in Oxford, and elsewhere. Particularly, we wish to thank Professor John Burrow, Dr. Anne Hudson, and Professor Derek Pearsall for their close readings of the edition and for their invaluable advice; we do not, however, mean to imply that they support our hypothesis, which remains our own responsibility.

George Rigg
Charlotte Brewer

Abbreviations

A	*Piers Plowman*, **A**-text/version; see p. 1 note 1.
B	*Piers Plowman*, **B**-text/version; see p. 1 note 1.
BL	British Library, London
C	*Piers Plowman*, **C**-text/version; see p. 1 note 1.
ME	Middle English
MED	*Middle English Dictionary* (Ann Arbor, 1952 – ; A-Neigh.).
Mustanoja	Tauno F. Mustanoja, *A Middle English Syntax*, Part I: *Parts of Speech* (Helsinki, 1960).
OE	Old English
OED	*Oxford English Dictionary*
OF	Old French
Pr	Prologue
Q	Scribe *Q* in MS Bodley 851 ; see pp. 6, 27-30.
Q^1	Section Q^1 of MS Bodley 851 ; see pp. 6, 27-30.
Q^2	Section Q^2 of MS Bodley 851 ; see pp. 6, 27-28.
X	Scribe *X* in MS Bodley 851 ; see pp. 3, 5.
Z	*Piers Plowman*, **Z**-text/version as found in MS Bodley 851.

For the manuscript abbreviations for the **A**, **B** and **C** texts, consult the editions listed in p. 1 note 1. Standard abbreviations are used for parts of speech.

Introduction

The version of *Piers Plowman* printed here for the first time (from the unique copy in MS Bodley 851) has considerable intrinsic interest and is, we believe, of great significance for the genesis of the poem. It consists of the first two "Visions" only, corresponding to A-text Prologue and Passus I-VIII (= **B** Prologue and Passus I-VII, **C** Passus I-X).[1] In "shape" it is closest to the A-text, but differs from it considerably. It is, for example, shorter: the corresponding part of **A** consists of 1791 lines (excluding Latin), whereas this version (henceforth known as **Z**)[2] has 1614 lines (including Latin). Not only does **Z** lack many long passages found in **A**, but it also has many unique passages not in **A**, as well as unique lines and unique readings for words and phrases. It is not textually related to any single manuscript of **A** or group of manuscripts. It contains (as do some **A** manuscripts) some lines otherwise peculiar to the **B** and/or **C** versions of the poem; it also contains many readings peculiar to **B** and/or **C**. **Z**'s peculiarities can be explained in two ways: *either* (Skeat, Kane)[3] it is derived from the A-text (with some contamination from the **B** and **C** traditions) and has been extensively modified by a compiler, who, from choice or necessity, omitted some passages, wrote some passages and lines of his own, and substituted his own readings; *or* (our view) **Z** represents a version of the poem *anterior* to the A-text.

Our reasons for this interpretation are set forth in the following pages. Briefly, they consist in: the internal coherence of the **Z** version, which can (with one or two exceptions, to be dealt with below)[4] be read as a self-

---

[1] **A** refers to *Piers Plowman: the A Version*, ed. George Kane (London, 1960); **B** refers to *Piers Plowman: the B Version*, ed. George Kane and E. Talbot Donaldson (London, 1975) – also referred to as Kane-Donaldson. **A** and **B** often indicate the agreed readings of **A** or **B** MSS, not necessarily the reading adopted by Kane or Kane-Donaldson. For the C-text we have used *The Vision of William concerning Piers the Plowman in Three Parallel Texts*, ed. W. W. Skeat, 2 vols. (Oxford, 1886; reprinted with addition of bibliography, 1954). Reference is also made to *Langland: Piers Plowman, Prologue and Passus I-VII of the B text*, ed. J. A. W. Bennett (Oxford, 1972).

[2] **Z** is the siglum used by Skeat and Kane to refer to MS Bodley 851.

[3] See below, pp. 9-12.

[4] See below, pp. 13-14.

sufficient and satisfying poem; the integrity of the language, which shows no signs of patching and which gives the solid impression of a West-Midland original with an overlay of non-Western spelling habits; the probable early date of the manuscript; the fact that **Z**'s peculiarities can all be explained more satisfactorily as early and rejected readings than as corruptions of the **A**-text; and finally, and most important, the difficulties in the alternative explanation, which requires (in our view) an improbable set of circumstances and procedures. Even if our interpretation is not accepted, however, we believe that the **Z**-version of *Piers Plowman* is sufficiently interesting to be considered in its own right, as a "scribal version," rather than to be relegated to the *apparatus criticus* of some future edition – for hitherto it has not achieved even this limited recognition.[5]

A. THE MANUSCRIPT

1. Physical Description

MS Bodley 851[6] is a parchment manuscript, measuring approximately 235-245 × 175-180 mm. It was first compiled in the late fourteenth century from two originally separate booklets (Parts I and II) and a third (Part III(a)) written by the compiler himself; it was later supplemented, in the fifteenth century.

Part I (fols. 7-77, quires iii-viii) contains Walter Map, *De Nugis Curialium*.

---

[5] It was not used by Skeat or Kane, and is not mentioned by Thomas A. Knott and David C. Fowler, *Piers the Plowman: a Critical Edition of the A-Version* (Baltimore, 1952). G. H. Russell describes it as a scribally corrupted version of the poem – "Some Aspects of the Process of Revision in *Piers Plowman*," in *Piers Plowman: Critical Approaches*, ed. S. S. Hussey (London, 1969), pp. 27-49 ; its C-text section is mentioned briefly by R. W. Chambers, "The Manuscripts of *Piers Plowman* in the Huntington Library, and Their Value for Fixing the Text of the Poem," *Huntington Library Bulletin* 8 (1935) 1-27. In the present edition **Z**, strictly speaking, refers to this version of the poem, not to this copy of it (whose scribe is designated *X*); for convenience, however, **Z** is often used to mean both version and text, unless there is a need to distinguish them; the Q-conclusion (below, pp. 27-30) is treated similarly.

[6] F. Madan and H. H. E. Craster, *A Summary Catalogue of Western Manuscripts in the Bodleian Library at Oxford* 2 (Oxford, 1922), no. 3041. For a full account of the manuscript, see A. G. Rigg, "Medieval Latin Poetic Anthologies (II)," *Mediaeval Studies* 40 (1978) 387-407; the present account is a summary of the main points in the article, with the important revision that the manuscript was probably compiled and written at Oxford rather than Ramsey (below, pp. 4-5). The article (p. 387) lists earlier descriptions by M. R. James and R. L. Poole and by E. Faral.

Part II (fols. 78-123, quires ix-xii) contains Latin poems, the longest of which is the *Speculum Stultorum*; some writing by the hand of Part I.

Part III (fols. 124-139, quires xiii-xiv) contains the **Z**-text of *Piers Plowman*. Hand *X*, the scribe of Part III (probably John Wells),[7] made additional entries in Parts I and II, had the manuscript decorated, and added the first set of flyleaves (fols. 5-6, quire ii, originally four leaves), on the last verso of which he drew his *ex libris* inscription.[8]

In the fifteenth century another set of flyleaves (fols. 1-4, quire i) was added; also a set of quires (fols. 140-208, quires xv-xxiii) was added to Part III to take a **C**-text of *Piers Plowman*.[9] Blank leaves throughout the manuscript were filled with numerous poems. Quire numbers (excluding quire i) were added.

Our concern is with Part III(a). These two quires, xiii^8-xiv^8, were originally separate, as is shown by the quire letters in the second quire: fols. 132-135 are numbered "b," "b ij," "b iij" and "b iiij" on the recto side. There are, on average, 50 lines per page. The Prologue and each Passus (except v) have a decorated initial in the style of the initials in Parts I and II. Hand *X* breaks off at the foot of fol. 139r, before the end of Passus VIII.[10] Part III(b) was made up by adding nine quires (fols. 140-208, quires xv^6-xvii^6, xviii^8, xix^{10}, xx^8-xxiii^8); its scribe, hand *Q*, completed Passus VIII, added a colophon, and then wrote out *Dowel, Dobet* and *Dobest* from a text close to the **C**-version (**C** XI-XXIII). These extra quires were presumably purchased as a bloc, blank: each quire is numbered, fol. 140r "j," fol. 146r "ij," and so on. The decoration of Part III(b) differs from that of Parts I-III(a).

2. Ownership, Date and Provenance

On fol. 6v is an elaborate picture[11] bearing the *ex libris* inscription "Iste liber constat Fratri Iohanni de Wellis Monacho Rameseye"; this seems to be by hand *X*, the scribe of Part III(a) (and of other poems in Parts I and II)

---

[7] See below, pp. 3-5.

[8] See note 11 below.

[9] See below, pp. 27-28.

[10] See below, pp. 27-30.

[11] "The name WELLIS is written in large scrolls; a lion on the left side pulls with his chain at the bow of the W; on the right side St. Christopher carries the Christ-child, and his staff pierces the S. Extensions of the ascenders of the W contain the words 'Iste liber constat Fratri Iohanni de' and those of the LL have 'Monacho Rameseye'." (Rigg, "Medieval Latin Poetic Anthologies (II)," p. 388). The fullest account is given by M. R. James (see note 6 above).

and compiler. John Wells[12] was a prominent opponent of Wycliffe; he
was a scholar of Gloucester College, Oxford, before 1376 and *prior
studentium* (1381); he was a vigorous participant in the council at Black
Friars in 1382, and was appointed proctor on behalf of the provincial
chapter of English Black Monks to go to Rome to plead for the release of
Cardinal Adam Easton; he died in Perugia in 1388. Tanner[13] quotes from
a chronicle in BL MS Otho D. viii (*ad finem*):

> A.D. MCCCLXXXVIII apud Perusiam obiit ven. doctor et malleus haereticorum
> mag. Ioh. Welleys, monachus Ramseye, sacrae theologiae professor, et in
> curia Romana totius ordinis monastici procurator; qui per tresdecim annos
> prior studentium Oxoniae, deinde electus in procuratorem ab incepcione
> sua anno xi in ecclesia S. Sabinae Perusiae est sepultus.

With so common a name, it is impossible to be certain that the prominent
Benedictine is the same person as the John Wells of the manuscript, but
probability favours the identification: this is the only John Wells of
Ramsey known at this period, and the Oxford connections of the manuscript[14] strengthen the argument for identification. It is equally impossible
to be certain that scribe *X* and John Wells are the same person, but again it
is likely: this is a private book, an anthology of satire and poems, and was
almost certainly compiled (from existing booklets) and/or copied by the
person whose name it bears. Part III(a) can therefore be dated between
1376 (or earlier) and 1388. The script, a neat Anglicana Formata, entirely
lacking any Secretary features, also supports a date in the later fourteenth
century.

   Although Wells came from Ramsey, there are good reasons for
thinking that the manuscript was compiled and written in Oxford. The *De
coniuge non ducenda* (Part II, No. 7) is textually very close indeed to the
copies in two other manuscripts: Trinity College, Cambridge, O.9.38 (s.
xv, written by a monk of Glastonbury)[15] and BL Cotton Vespasian E. xii (s.
xv, owned by John Russell, Bishop of Lincoln and Chancellor of

---

   [12] For biographies of Wells, see the article by T. F. Tout in the *Dictionary of National
Biography* and especially A. B. Emden, *A Biographical Register of the University of Oxford
to 1500*, 3 vols. (Oxford, 1957-1959), s.v., and articles cited there. Emden hesitated about
identifying the owner of Bodley 851 as the famous anti-Wycliffite, because of the
fifteenth-century items in the manuscript; all these entries, however, were made later than
the entries by hand *X* and the *ex libris* inscription.
   [13] Thomas Tanner, *Bibliotheca Britannico-Hibernica* (London, 1748), p. 757.
   [14] See below.
   [15] See A. G. Rigg, *A Glastonbury Miscellany of the Fifteenth Century* (Oxford, 1968);
the proposal that this manuscript was written in Oxford is a recent idea (see next note).

Oxford).[16] The obvious meeting place for all three (i.e., the place where each would have been copied from a common exemplar) is Oxford, perhaps Gloucester College itself, the Oxford *locus* for Benedictines of Ramsey and Glastonbury. Wells was certainly an Oxford man for most of his active life and his title in the bookplate, "monk of Ramsey," does not have to mean that he was in Ramsey when the manuscript was written. Another anthology, Digby 166, was compiled from booklets apparently sold by a bookseller, possibly in Oxford, certainly in a university:[17] Wells may have obtained the nucleus of Bodley 851 (i.e., Parts I and II) in a similar way. To summarize, the **Z**-text of *Piers Plowman*, Part III(a) of Bodley 851, was probably written in Oxford by John Wells of Ramsey Abbey and Gloucester College, some time between 1376 (or earlier) and 1388.

Among the fifteenth-century additions is a series of verses and proverbs on the front flyleaves, many signed "Dodsthorp"; although one or two of these entries show an interest in Ramsey, there is no reason to suppose that the manuscript left Oxford – other Ramsey monks may have found it at Gloucester College and made entries in it. One of the entries is an epitaph of John Wells:[18]

> O benedicte pie, prece virginis alme marie,
> Venturis annis Wellis memorare Iohannis:
> Doctor erat gratus, prudens, pius, hic tumulatus.
> Moribus ornatus, venerans fuit et veneratus.

Unless this is fictitious, the words "hic tumulatus" imply that it is a copy of the inscription on his tomb at Perugia.[19]

B. THE *PIERS PLOWMAN* TEXTS IN MS BODLEY 851

At this point a review of the nature of the texts of *Piers Plowman* in this manuscript will be useful.

On fols. 124r-139r is the **Z**-text, written by hand *X* (probably John Wells); it extends from the Prologue to Passus VIII 92 (= **A** VIII 88). It occupies two quires (originally separate from the rest of the manuscript),

---

[16] See A. G. Rigg, "Medieval Latin Poetic Anthologies (III)," *Mediaeval Studies* 41 (1979) 468-505, where the Oxford origin of several anthologies is discussed.

[17] Ibid. pp. 473-474, 505.

[18] "Medieval Latin Poetic Anthologies (II)," Appendix No. 3, p. 403.

[19] If Bodley 851 remained in Oxford, the *terminus a quo* of 1439 suggested for the fifteenth-century flyleaf entries (established by the Visitation of the Bishop of Alnwick) is removed.

xiii^8-xiv^8, and ends near the bottom of the recto side of the last leaf of quire xiv. This text is printed here, pp. 39-110.

A fifteenth-century scribe, hand Q, added nine more quires, xv-xxiii (probably purchased blank in a bloc). He completed Passus vIII, beginning immediately where X left off on fol. 139r and ending near the bottom of fol. 140v (the first leaf of the first of the new quires). He added a final couplet and colophon. This section is referred to here as Q^1 and is printed below, pp. 110-114.

The same scribe Q, beginning on fol. 141r, now wrote out a text of *Dowel, Dobet* and *Dobest* according to the C-version (**C** xi-xxiii), ending on fol. 208r. This is referred to here as Q^2 and is not printed here.

Most of this Introduction concerns **Z**, but section Q^1 is also important: for example, were **Z** and Q^1 copied from the same exemplar?[20] There is no doubt that section Q^2 is from a separate source: although the combination of **A** Prologue and Passus i-vIII with **C** xi-xxiii is also found in the National Library of Wales ms No. 773B[21] there is no reason to think that this combination is in any way authorial – each scribe may have independently decided, after writing the end of the *Visio* (i.e., the end of **A** Passus vIII) that he should switch to a longer conclusion, i.e., the **C**-text.

C. NARRATIVE SEQUENCE OF THE **Z** VERSION

1. Basic Plot of **Z**, **A** and **B**

The action of the first two "Visions" (Prologue and Passus i-vIII in **Z** and **A**, Prologue and Passus i-vII in **B**) is essentially the same in **Z**, **A** and **B**.

First Vision

The dreamer sees a tower on a hill and a deep dale beneath; between the two is a "fair field of folk," described in their various occupations. Holy Church instructs the dreamer on the nature of the tower of Truth. When asked to define falsehood, she indicates Lady Meed. Meed is about to be married to False, but the king is informed and temporarily suspends the ceremony; he attempts to marry Meed to Conscience, but Conscience will have none of it. An illustrative episode follows: Peace denounces Wrong for various wrong-doings, but Peace is in time persuaded to accept monetary compensation from Meed. Reason denounces the power of Meed at court; the king agrees and the vision ends (at the beginning of Passus v).

---

[20] See below, pp. 28-30.
[21] Described by Kane, **A**-text, pp. 12-13.

Second Vision

In response to Conscience's sermon (Reason's in **B**) the various Sins make their confessions and pledge to seek Truth. They need a guide, and Piers Plowman says that he knows Truth well; he will guide them, but first must plough his half-acre. The people assist him, but eventually grow lazy. They are forced back to work by Hunger, whose appetite grows so great as to cause starvation. Piers ponders on the difficulty of keeping a balance between Hunger and slothfulness. In reward for his good work Piers and the pilgrims are given a pardon by Truth, which is described in detail. (**Z** ends here and section Q^1 begins.) The validity of the pardon is questioned by a priest. Here ends the second vision, which is followed by the dreamer's reflections on the value of indulgences and the validity of dreams.

2. DIFFERENCES IN NARRATIVE BETWEEN **Z**, AND **AB**

The major differences in narrative are as follows:[22]

(1) At Pr 17 **Z** does not mention the dungeon (referred to at Pr 100).

(2) **Z** differs frequently from **A** and **B** on the order of occupations in the "fair field"; it lacks the ecclesiastics (**A** Pr 90-95), the pardoner-priest episode (**A** Pr 77-79), and the cooks (**A** Pr 104-108), and is shorter in many places. Conversely, **Z** has two sections not in **AB**: bishops, etc. (**Z** Pr 53-58) and judges (**Z** Pr 70-73). **B** has two major expansions from **A** (**B** Pr 87-111 and 112-210).

(3) In **Z** the Prologue does not end until Holy Church has begun her teaching.

(4) At **Z** II 163-170 Conscience gives a résumé of the action in the Meed-False marriage; this is not in **AB**.

(5) In **AB** Passus II ends with the capture of Meed; in **Z** (II 214-215) both Meed and Flattery are captured, which is contradicted by **Z** III 1.

(6) In **A** (**A** III 34-89) Meed, after arriving at court, is shriven by a friar in return for a promise to build a window, and the poet criticizes mayors for failing to regulate retail trade (expanded in **B** III 35-100); this passage is lacking in **Z**.

(7) At the end of Passus III all three versions differ: in **Z** (**Z** III 147-176) Meed accuses Conscience of miserliness, even avarice, and says that he is at the root of human decisions, right or wrong. In **A** (**A** III 196-276) Conscience defines the difference between Meed and right reward; in **B** (III 209-353) the passage is similar to **A**, but much longer.

---

[22] See Table of Concordance, pp. 128-137.

(8) In Passus IV (**Z** IV 122-130), **Z** has a sharp interchange between the king and Reason, in which Reason demands the removal of Meed from court. This passage (not in this position in **AB**) makes good sense in context, but is repeated in slightly different words (closer to those of **A**) at the beginning of Passus V (**Z** V 1-9). In **AB** the passage is placed in this later position (**A** IV 141-149).

(9) At the end of Passus IV in **Z** (**Z** IV 158-159), the king and Reason leave, and the dreamer says that he "saw them no more"; they are, in fact, still present at the beginning of Passus V.

(10) In **AB** Passus V begins somewhat later than in **Z**. **B** here has several expansions from **A**.

(11) After mention of the south-west wind **Z** has a brief digression (**Z** V 34-40) on "word is but wind" and the Word of God; this is not in **AB**.

(12) In **Z** most of the confessions of the Sins are much shorter than those in **A** (which in turn are shorter than those in **B**).[23] **A** lacks Wrath, which is linked with Envy in **Z** and has a full confession in **B** (**B** V 135-187).

(13) In **Z** Robert the Robber concludes his confession with three lines (**Z** V 142-144) based on the parable of the Wicked Steward; these lines are not in **AB**.

(14) **A** begins Passus VI somewhat earlier than **Z** (at **Z** V 155); **B** differs entirely, by absorbing the whole of Passus VI into Passus V.

(15) **Z** has several lines (**Z** VI 68-75) on the "natural powers" of Truth; two of these lines are in **A** (**A** VI 80, 81), but none are in **B**.

(16) Some lines on the Tower of Truth (**Z** VI 76-78) are peculiar to **Z**; two lines (**Z** VI 79-80) are in **BC** but only in four **A** manuscripts.

(17) At the end of the Passus, **A** has a long section (**A** VI 104-123) beginning with an account of the Seven Sisters that serve Truth (expanded in **B**); this passage is not in **Z**.

(18) **Z** lacks the list of exceptions to the workers who will be allowed to glean at harvest-time (**A** VII 62-69).

(19) The name of Piers' son (**Z** VII 64 ff.) differs entirely from that in **A** (VII 72 ff.).

(20) **Z** has a short passage on the needy (**Z** VII 196-201), which is not in **AB** but is similar to an earlier one in **ZAB** (**Z** VII 127-128) and to a later one which is in **AB** but not in **Z** (**A** VII 208-212).

(21) **Z** has a long satirical attack on doctors (**Z** VII 260-278); this is not in **AB**, which have only two lines on the subject (**A** VII 257-258).

---

[23] See below, p. 18.

The main difference between **Z** and **A**, however, consists not so much in the major substitutions listed above but in constant textual differences, in the order of lines,[24] in wording and phrasing, and in the presence or absence of relatively unimportant lines. In many cases **Z** shares these features with **B** and/or **C** (against **A**),[25] but usually **Z**'s differences are unique.

D. EXPLANATIONS OF Z'S PECULIARITIES

1. SKEAT'S AND KANE'S INTERPRETATION

Skeat came across Bodley 851 too late to use it in his edition of the **A**-text, mainly, it seems, because it lacks certain key passages that he was using for comparison between the manuscripts. By the time he edited the **C**-text he had seen the manuscript and gave a full, if somewhat bemused, account of it.[26] His view is adequately summarized in his words in the Three-Text edition: "The former part [i.e., Passus I-VIII] is mere rubbish, written out from imperfect recollection." [27] Skeat did not make a detailed textual analysis of it. Kane's account, though no less damning, is more careful and systematic:[28]

> The editor of **A** takes the opportunity of mentioning in this category [i.e., rejected manuscripts of the **B**-text] Bodleian Library MS 851 (S.C. 3041) which he rightly dismissed as worthless for editorial use, but should have formally rejected in Vol. I. This is the manuscript called Z by Skeat (*C-Text*, pp. xxx-xxxiii).
>
> Z is a conjoint manuscript. Its earlier part, to fol. 140b, is a conflated and sophisticated text resembling **A** more than **B** or **C**. There is no doubt that its origin was in the **A** tradition. It has also an unmistakable element of **C** version lines and a few lines and readings characteristic of **B**. That part of the text which is referable to **A** is much disordered and lacks many lines and passages. The passus are most often misdivided, apparently by guess.

---

[24] In the Q[1] section also the line-order differs from **A**, but this results solely from Q's misplacing of the Latin quotations.

[25] See below, pp. 20-25. Some **A** MSS occasionally behave like **Z** in this respect.

[26] W. W. Skeat, *The Vision of William Concerning Piers the Plowman*, Part III [= Text **C**], Early English Text Society, o.s. 54 (1873), Introduction, pp. xxx-xxxiii. Skeat quotes a few passages from **Z** and comments on the Norfolk allusions.

[27] Skeat, *Three Parallel Texts* edition, vol. 2, Introduction, p. lxxi (no. XXXI).

[28] Kane's statement is in the Kane-Donaldson edition of the **B**-text, pp. 14-15, note 95. Similar views are expressed in G. H. Russell, "Some Aspects of the Process of Revision in *Piers Plowman*," in *Piers Plowman: Critical Approaches*, ed. S. S. Hussey (London, 1969), pp. 27-49, especially p. 28.

The text there contains many lines not relatable to any version, thus presumably spurious, and some of these occur at points of omission, as where the confessions of Envy and Avarice are reduced to 13 lines of which ten are peculiar to Z (see Skeat, op. cit., pp. xxxi, xxxii). In the latter part, that is on fols 141ff. from Skeat's **C** xɪ 1 onward, it reads like a good text of **C**.

The significant features of the first part are the extremely uneven quality of its text, which for short stretches can be quite good, the large amount of omission, the frequent disordering of lines, producing an imperfect or wholly inconsequent exposition, and the circumstance that some of the groups of "new" lines occur where approximate multiples of 20 or 40 lines are wanting (i.e., the presumptive contents of sides or leaves). One possibility is that the early part of Z was copied from a text produced by someone acquainted with all versions of the poem, literate and able to write tolerable long lines, who was restoring from memory, and occasionally by sophistication, a physically very defective copy, very imperfect, or in many places defaced, or both, of the **A** version. The other possibility is that the whole of the "**A**" component of the manuscript is merely a memorial reconstruction, the uneven quality of the text and the occasional coincidences of omission with sophistication being simply results of uneven recollection.

Apart from the fact that we have observed no sign of the "approximate multiples of 20 or 40 lines" (supposedly missing), Kane's account is a perfectly possible, if somewhat complicated, explanation for the peculiarities of **Z**.[29] Our reasons for rejecting it are as follows:

(1) Textual: The textual evidence (the presence in **Z** of **B/C** lines and the relationship of **Z** with the manuscript tradition of the **A**-text) is, in fact, neutral: it can be used to support Kane's position or ours. The **B/C** lines may be the result of conflation/contamination (either textual or memorial) by a scribe who is essentially trying to write out an **A**-text, or (our view) may be integral to the original draft of the poem, omitted by manuscripts of the **A**-tradition. The implications of our hypothesis are set out below (pp. 20-25), but we should note here that the **B/C** lines nowhere interrupt the thought or syntax of the **Z** narrative. Kane lists manuscripts of the **A**-text which contain lines from the **B** or **C** texts;[30] we would argue that those lines shared with **Z** are part of the first draft of the poem and that

---

[29] Some of the textual and linguistic evidence (discussed below) requires that the "restoration" of a physically defective copy or the "memorial reconstruction" should have taken place at a stage earlier than the copying of Bodley 851; this is not of itself, of course, an objection to Kane's explanation of **Z**.

[30] Kane, A-text, pp. 30-31.

their presence in some **A** manuscripts can be explained either as representing the genuine tradition or as coincidence. Certainly some **A** manuscripts are independently contaminated by **B** and/or **C**: most of the lines listed by Kane are not in **Z**. Manuscripts W and N, for example, have a great number of **B** and **C** lines which are not in **Z**. **Z** Pr 5, which resembles a **C** line, is also in manuscript K, but K is otherwise recognizably contaminated by **C**. There is, however, no sign that **Z** is the result of contamination or conflation. One manuscript of the **B**-text, Huntington 114, has been shown to be the result of conflation on a large scale:[31] marks of joining, repetitions, etc. confirm Russell's and Nathan's opinion that it was "made by one who had before him all three texts of the poem." **Z** betrays no such signs of conflation.

Z cannot be placed firmly within any one family of manuscripts of the **A**-text: it agrees disjunctively with each of 12 of the 17 manuscripts of the **A**-text, and at some time agrees with each of all the major families of manuscripts.[32] This fact is also neutral: deliberate conflation is unlikely, but **Z** is certainly not unique in containing readings from all of the textual traditions of **A**. On the other hand, its textual behaviour can equally well be interpreted in our favour (see below, p. 25).

Z's most distinctive feature, of course, is its unique lines and passages. Kane lists the additional lines found in manuscripts of the **A**-texts:[33] none of these are found in **Z**, whose non-**A** lines are qualitatively quite different. Where the "additional lines" in the **A** manuscripts are brief and flat (often resembling the spurious links in manuscripts of the *Canterbury Tales*), those of **Z** are often extensive and poetically superior. Textual evidence alone, therefore, supports neither Kane's hypothesis nor ours: positive evidence must be sought in the nature and quality of **Z** itself.

(2) Literary: There are no signs of "patching" either where **Z** lacks passages found in **A** or where **Z** has material not in **A**. If **Z** had been "cobbled" from a defective exemplar, one would expect to see signs of the "joins": the few inconsistencies in **Z** do not occur at the major points of "omission" or "addition." Although the quality of the "spurious" passages varies, many of them seem to us to be beyond the capacity of someone merely "literate and able to write tolerable long lines." [34] The coherence of

---

[31] G. H. Russell and Venetia Nathan, "A *Piers Plowman* Manuscript in the Huntington Library," *Huntington Library Quarterly* 26 (1963) 119-130; see also Kane-Donaldson, pp. 14-15, and Chambers (cited in note 5 above). We have not seen the manuscript or a copy of it; our information is taken from the Russell-Nathan article.

[32] See below, pp. 23-24.

[33] Kane, **A**-text, pp. 44-50.

[34] Kane, cited above, p. 10.

the narrative makes it easier to believe that **A** is an expanded revision of **Z** rather than that **Z** is an abridgment of **A**.

(3) Linguistic: The text of **Z** is linguistically totally coherent and uniform, in spelling, morphology, syntax and vocabulary: the lines and passages peculiar to **Z** show no signs of being alien to the parts shared with **A**.[35] Such consistency goes deeper than would be expected from a sophisticated scribal pastiche.

(4) Dating: If Bodley 851 was written before 1388 (probably well before), as argued above, this seems a very early date for the diffusion of all versions in such a way as to produce conflation on this scale.

(5) The existence of an alternative explanation: namely, that **Z** represents a version of the poem anterior to **A** and is thus textually independent of all other versions. This hypothesis will now be presented in detail.

2. The Hypothesis that **Z** Precedes **A**

We believe that **Z** presents a coherent and self-sufficient version of the poem. Apart from the inconsistencies already mentioned[36] (to be discussed below), we do not believe that the "disordering of lines" produces "an imperfect or wholly inconsequent exposition."[37] On the contrary, we believe that Kane's judgment of **Z** passages as "good" or "spurious" is based largely on the assumption that **A** preserves the "correct" reading, not on the innate characteristics of the passages themselves.

(a) *General Remarks*

A few general points should be made first. Many medieval texts are extant in two versions, one longer, one shorter. Sometimes the author tells us which is which: Berchorius informs us that the longer version of his *Ovidius moralizatus* is his revised and expanded work.[38] Sometimes we depend on the scribe, whose reliability must be assessed: the colophon to the longer Paris text of Simon Chèvre d'Or's *Ylias* informs us that it is the revision.[39] Usually, however, we have no reliable information, either

---

[35] See below, pp. 26-27 and Appendix, pp. 115-127.

[36] See above, pp. 7-8, Nos. 1, 5, 8, 9.

[37] Kane, cited above, p. 10.

[38] Petrus Berchorius, *De formis figurisque deorum*, Werkmateriaal (3), ed. J. Engels (Utrecht, 1966), p. 3, Prologue, fols. 1rb43-1va4.

[39] A. Boutemy, "La version parisienne du poème de Simon Chèvre d'Or sur la guerre de Troie (MS lat. 8430)," *Scriptorium* 1 (1946-1947) 267-288; colophon on p. 286.

external or internal, and must rely on our own judgment to decide whether the longer text is an authorial expansion of the shorter or the shorter is an authorial (or scribal) abridgment of the longer. The shorter versions of Walter of Wimborne's Latin poems are interpreted by the editor as scribal abridgments.[40] Opinions vary on whether Chaucer produced two editions of *Troilus* or whether texts lacking certain passages are simply deficient.[41] In the present case we believe that just as **A** is anterior to **B**, so **Z** is anterior to **A** – and for similar reasons. Arguing for the antecedence of **A** to **B** and **C** Kane and Donaldson write:[42]

> ... we will assert that the **A** version has no literary qualities which would justify considering it the work of anyone but a major poet. We find in it the integral characteristics of a substantive work of art, a poem free, except for scribal damage, of the marks of debasement inevitably left by an inferior talent reducing that which itself it could not have created.

This precisely summarizes our view of **Z**. In many cases our arguments are similar to those used by Kane and by Kane-Donaldson in establishing the **A** and **B** texts: **Z** frequently preserves an "older" linguistic form or a manifest *difficilior lectio*. **Z**'s individual readings are rarely of a kind likely to be introduced by scribal interference.[43] Bodley 851, of course, is only a copy of the **Z**-version: it has its own share of scribal damage of the usual kind.[44]

(b) *Draft Nature of* **Z**

The evidence suggests that **Z** was still in draft form or represents a partial revision of the earliest version of the poem: the few inconsistencies in the narrative are better explained thus rather than as corruptions of **A**.

(1) The failure to mention the dungeon (**Z** Pr 17) is not necessarily an inconsistency: when Holy Church mentions it (**Z** Pr 100) she does not imply that the dreamer has already noticed it. On the other hand, the poet may have decided, in revision, to provide an early reference to the dungeon.[45]

---

[40] *The Poems of Walter of Wimborne*, ed. A. G. Rigg (Toronto, 1978), pp. 10-12.

[41] *The Book of Troilus and Criseyde by Geoffrey Chaucer*, ed. Robert Kilburn Root (Princeton, 1945), pp. lxx-lxxxi. For a contrary view, see B. Windeatt, "The Text of Troilus," in *Essays on Troilus and Criseyde*, ed. M. Salu (Cambridge, 1979), pp. 1-22.

[42] Kane-Donaldson, **B**-text, p. 73.

[43] See below, pp. 15-17, 26-27, 123-124, 126-127.

[44] See below, pp. 30-31.

[45] The dungeon is not mentioned in the **C**-text at all.

(2) Two related pieces of "incoherence" are seen at the end of Passus ɪv and the beginning of Passus v.[46] A nine line passage appears twice (at **Z** ɪv 122-130 and v 1-9) and at the beginning of Passus v the king and Reason are still present, although the dreamer has just said (**Z** ɪv 158-159) that he "saw them no more." This confusion could hardly have arisen from corruption of the **A**-text: if the scribe had inadvertently copied v 1-9 in the wrong place (i.e., too early), why would he then compound his error by writing three "new" lines (**Z** ɪv 157-159) which would be immediately contradicted by the opening words of the "correct" passage in Passus v ? Our suggestion is that Langland originally put the interchange between the king and Reason in its earlier position (at **Z** ɪv 122-130) and intended to end the First Vision at the end of the Passus (hence the concluding lines in **Z** ɪv 157-159). He then decided to transfer the interchange to the beginning of Passus v and to continue the dream for a few lines more. The present copy of **Z** was then made before Langland went back and cancelled ɪv 122-130 and ɪv 157-159. Support for this theory may be seen in the phrase *quaþ resoun* in **A** ɪv 117: in this position in **Z** it introduces Reason's speech (**Z** ɪv 132) but may be purely vestigial in **A**, where this is no longer the beginning of the speech. (On the other hand, cf., e.g., **B** ɪɪɪ 59.) Further, the wording of **Z** v 1-9 is closer to **A** than **Z** ɪv 122-130; this suggests that the earlier passage is also the older.

(3) A minor piece of uncancelled inconsistency is the mention of Flattery at the end of Passus ɪɪ (214-215): Meed is alone at the beginning of the next Passus (i.e., in the next line). That an author would forget to cancel an earlier idea is perfectly understandable; that a scribe should introduce an inconsistency immediately before a line which would contradict it is much less probable.

(4) At **Z** ɪ 101-102 what at first sight appears to be a totally corrupt line can be interpreted as a partial translation of the Latin text: the **A**-text gives the Latin in full and completes (and corrects) the translation. (The apparent corruption at ɪ 79-80 could be a similar sign of an unfinished line, but more probably results from incorrect line-division.)

(5) There are many examples of cases where **Z**'s reading, perfectly acceptable in itself, explains a reading in manuscripts of **A**: e.g., v 129. See also vɪ 30 and note.

(c) *Passus Divisions*

The Passus divisions in **Z** differ from those in **A** – between Prologue and Passus ɪ, Passus ɪv and v, and v and vɪ. In each case the **A** division is

---

[46] See above, p. 8, Nos. 8-9.

superior: it is clearly better to separate Holy Church's teaching from the "field of folk" and to separate the search for Truth from the preliminary repentance of sins (though in **B** and **C** there is no division at all between Passus v and vi). Certainly no "sophisticated" scribe would deliberately alter **A**'s divisions to those of **Z**. On the other hand, **Z**'s divisions are quite acceptable and need not be regarded as errors or the result of guesswork.[47]

(d) *Lines and Passages Peculiar to* **Z**[48]

(1) Longer passages with no counterpart in **A** include: Pr 53-58 (bishops, etc.), Pr 70-73 (judges), ii 163-170 (Conscience's résumé of Meed's activities), v 34-40 ("word is but wind"), v 142-144 ("I cannot dig"), vi 68-75 (natural powers of Truth), vii 260-278 (satire against doctors). These passages do not occur "at points of omission" from **A**: if **Z** is interpreted as the result of scribal interference, these passages must be regarded as unmotivated imitations. They seem to us to be so Langlandian in style and content as to be beyond the capabilities of an imitator. This is a subjective judgment, and cannot be proved one way or the other. An anonymous reader of the **Z**-text has written of such passages: "What makes them 'Langlandian' for me is that they are unexpected, knotty, difficult and rewarding to think about." Particularly striking is the skill with which Robert the Robber (v 142-144) plays on the Latin word *cautionem* from Luc. 16:1-13 ("*caute* wold Y make") and integrates the Latin into the alliterative pattern ("For *fodere non valeo*, so feble ar my bones"); compare **Z** viii 61, where **Z** has *mercedem* (from the earlier Latin quotation) against **A**'s *mede*. Similarly effective is **Z** v 34-40, in which the reference to the south-west wind is extended (via a proverb) into an image for the power of God's word. The natural powers of Truth (vi 68-75) and the satire against physicians with the topical allusion to Lombardy's reputation for poisoning (vii 260-278) seem to us also well beyond an imitator's skills. The one noticeably weak passage is Conscience's résumé (ii 163-170), which is a pastiche of earlier lines describing Meed's activities; it seems to be only half-written, with several syntactic anacolutha (and is also corrupt). On the other hand, there is no reason to believe that it is not Langland's: he may have thought that some kind of summary was necessary at this point and patched one together, and then later realized that it was not needed and cancelled it.

---

[47] Langland's practice on ending visions varies: the dreamer awakes at the end of **B** Passus xvii and xix, but at the beginning of **B** Passus xiii. On the use of capitulum marks in **Z**, which sometimes coincide with the beginnings of A Passus, see below, p. 32.

[48] For passages peculiar to **Z** but with corresponding (longer) passages in **A**, see below, pp. 17-18.

(2) Not all **Z**'s unique lines are of high quality (though this does not mean that they are not authentic). It is easy to see why Langland would reject "And ye schal lyue the lengur by a long tyme" (**Z** vi 44) in favour of "And ȝe shuln lepe þe liȝtliere al ȝoure lif tyme" (**A** vi 56). Indeed, our whole hypothesis rests on the presumption that **Z** is "inferior" to **A**, just as **A** is presumed to be "inferior" to **B** simply to account for the writing of **B**.[49] Reasons for the rejection of particular **Z** lines and passages are not always easy to find, just as changes from **A** to **B** and from **B** to **C** are sometimes inexplicable. Some of **Z**'s passages are digressive; some are internally successful but allegorically disruptive (e.g., III 147-176). Most of the **Z** lines not found in **A**, **B** or **C** have no organic or textual significance. Some provide unnecessary transitions (II 1-3; IV 157-159; VII 230-232); some unnecessarily repeat or expand earlier lines or ideas (Pr 99-100, 145; I 18, 23, 39; II 10, 40-42, 47, 118, 163-170, 188-189; IV 119-121; V 73-75; VII 107-109, 238, 245); some seem to be mere padding (II 177; V 43, 70, 130; VII 31, 316; VIII 75-76); some seem to be experimental lines, perhaps originally intended for expansion but later cancelled (I 65; III 96; VII 48-49, 170).

(3) Sometimes one can see the progressive elimination of a theme from one version to another. The "natural powers" of Truth are described extensively in **Z** (VI 67-75); in **A** only two of these lines survive (**A** VI 80-81), and even these disappear in **B** and **C**. If the line has been correctly interpreted, **Z** (VII 165) has a character not in any other version, namely Sir Thirst (corresponding to Hunger); textual vestiges of his name can be seen in a few **A** manuscripts (see note), but he has disappeared entirely from **B** and **C**. The character Soothness appears four times in **Z** (II 45, 159; IV 50, 154); in **A** he survives only in the second and fourth instances (**Z** II 159 = **A** II 150, and **Z** IV 154 = **A** IV 138); in **B** and **C** he occurs in the second (i.e., **A** II 150 = **B** II 189) but has been restored to the fourth (**A** IV 138 = **B** IV 162) by Kane-Donaldson against the testimony of the **B** manuscripts. In **B** and **C** he also occurs in a new place (**B** II 24, **C** III 24), not in **AZ**.

(4) The Norfolk allusions: In **Z** III 148 Meed, denouncing Conscience for miserliness, says "Out of Northfolk or Normawndye thy name was yfounde"; in **Z** V 98 Covetousness is described as having "a Northfolk nose" and swears in a Norfolk dialect phrase. Neither line is retained in **A**,

---

[49] In the commentary attention is drawn to several places where **Z**'s reading has been replaced in **A** by one that is clearly superior – more vigorous, syntactically clearer, more precise, metrically smoother, less repetitious, etc.: Pr 80, 83; I 23, 116; II 146, 147, 160, 206; IV 24, 142; V 44; VII 107-108, 170; VIII 89-90. Readers will no doubt find others.

B or **C**, but at **B** v 236 Covetousness says "I kan no frenssh in feiþ but of þe ferþest ende of Northfolk," which Skeat and Bennett interpret as a comment on the linguistic provinciality of Norfolk; Bennett, however, also mentions the possibility of "a special allusion to the reputation for cheating and dishonesty enjoyed by the *baratores de Norfolchia*." The first two allusions, and probably the third, are part of a tradition of anti-Norfolk satire in the later Middle Ages. On the flyleaves of Bodley 851 is a proverb "Fallere gnarus homo Norfolchia venit ab humo." [50] The major example of the satire is the poem *Descriptio Northfolchie*,[51] copies of which are found in Trinity College, Cambridge, MS O.9.38, probably written in Oxford,[52] and in the related pair of manuscripts BL Cotton Titus A. xx and Bodleian Rawlinson B. 214.[53] Another example is Chaucer's Reeve (cf. **Z** v 99 note). Ridicule of isolated communities is common at all times: Newfoundlanders are often the butt of jokes ("Newfie jokes") by other Canadians. In the ninth century Frisians were considered barbaric and stupid by continental Europeans.[54] East Anglia was similarly isolated, both in geography and in mores, from the rest of England.[55] The textual evidence of the manuscripts mentioned above suggests that anti-Norfolk jokes may have been particularly current in Oxford.

(e) *Passages in* **A** *but not in* **Z**

Such passages are naturally labelled "omissions" by Kane, but in our view they are "passages not yet written." As noted above, we have not observed omissions in blocks of 20 or 40 lines. Further, none of the so-called "omissions" disturbs the narrative sequence: if they were the result of textual deficiency, one would expect some traces of inconsequentiality: such inconsequentialities as there are in **Z** (discussed above) do not occur at the points of omission. Significantly, many of the passages present in **A** but wanting in **Z** are longer in **B** (and sometimes longer still in **C**). This

[50] "Medieval Latin Poetic Anthologies (II)," Appendix No. 49, p. 405.
[51] Ed. T. Wright, *Early Mysteries and other Latin poems* (London, 1838), pp. 93-106; critical edition by A. G. Rigg, "An Edition of a Fifteenth-Century Commonplace Book," unpublished D.Phil. thesis (Oxford, 1966), 1: 146-156, 2: 356-370; see *Glastonbury Miscellany* (note 15 above), pp. 81-82. The thesis cited here gives other examples of similar satire, especially against Norfolk.
[52] See above, pp. 4-5, and "Medieval Latin Poetic Anthologies (III)," p. 505.
[53] See A. G. Rigg, "Medieval Latin Poetic Anthologies (I)," *Mediaeval Studies* 39 (1977) 281-330.
[54] William H. TeBrake, "Ecology and Economy in Early Medieval Frisia," *Viator* 9 (1978) 2-29.
[55] See George C. Homans, "The Frisians in East Anglia," *Economic History Review* 2nd series, 10 (1957-1958) 189-206; this reference was kindly supplied by Professor TeBrake.

suggests that certain parts of the poem were subjected to constant revision and expansion by Langland.[56]

(1) After **Z** III 36, **A** has the episode of Meed and the Friar and the discussion of retail trade (**A** III 34-89); this is expanded in **B** (III 35-100) and even further in **C** (IV 38-126).

(2) The end of Passus III in **Z** (**Z** III 147-176) is entirely altered in **A**, probably because Meed's denunciation of Conscience for avarice had got out of hand. The new passage in **A** is much longer (**A** III 196-276); in **B** it is longer still (**B** III 209-353), and yet longer in **C** (**C** IV 266-501).

(3) The confessions of the Sins seem to have been particularly subject to revision. In **Z** Envy and Wrath share six lines (**Z** v 91-96); in the process of expansion **A** extends Envy's confession considerably (**A** v 58-106), but omits Wrath entirely; **B** adds a little to Envy (**B** v 75-134) and supplies the missing Wrath (v 135-187); in **C** the confession of Envy is somewhat reduced. Covetousness is similarly expanded from **Z** (**Z** v 97-103) to **A** (**A** v 107-145) to **B** (**B** v 188-295); **C** is similar in length to **B**. Gluttony has six lines in **Z** (**Z** v 104-109), expanded considerably by **A** (**A** v 146-212) and again by **B** (**B** v 296-384); again, **C** resembles **B**. Sloth has much the same space in **Z** and **A** (**Z** v 110-130, **A** v 213-232) but has more in **B** (**B** v 385-460); **C** is similar to **B**.[57]

(4) At the end of Passus VI, after **Z** VI 102, **A** has a section on the Seven Sisters that serve Truth and the reaction of the pilgrims to Piers' description of the way to Truth (**A** VI 104-123). The latter passage is expanded in **B** (**B** v 630-642) and is slightly longer again in **C** (**C** VIII 292-306).

(5) Much of the expansion from **Z** to **A** consists in single lines, where **A** has either added a line or two or expanded a single line into two. The Table of Concordance provides examples.

The arguments succinctly stated by Kane-Donaldson[58] for the sequence **A** to **B** and **B** to **C** work in exactly the same way, *mutatis mutandis*, for **Z** to **A** and **A** to **B**.

(f) *Cruces in the* **A**-*text*

The **Z** version has a bearing on several major cruces of the **A**-text (sometimes affecting **B** and **C** also); these are all discussed more fully in the commentary.

---

[56] These are the passages that, according to Kane, "occur at points of omission" from **A**: see above, pp. 9-10.

[57] In the **B**-text many of the passages associated with the Sins are shifted to Passus XIII, another sign of Langland's constant tampering with this section.

[58] Kane-Donaldson, **B**-text, pp. 72-73; cf. above, p. 13.

(1) **Z** Pr 129 (**A** ı 39): here **Z**'s reading "and that seuth thy soule ant seyth in thyn herte" is certainly the *difficilior lectio*; it explains the corruption in various **B** manuscripts, but retains the sense that we see in **C**. Clearly the **A**-text is corrupt here.

(2) **Z** ı 86 (**A** ı 137): editors of **A** and **B** usually reject *plente* as an easy error, in favour of *plante*, but the phrase *plente of pes* has a biblical authority which is particularly appropriate at this point.

(3) **Z** ıı 94 agrees with **B** (**B** ıı 123) but is two lines in **A** (**A** ıı 86a-87); the **ZB** reading can be defended as the earlier, if not the superior, reading: the vocalic alliteration involving Latin could have caused the alteration in **A**.

(4) **Z** ııı 32-33: **Z** shares these "**C**-lines" with manuscripts W and N, which place them differently; Kane rejects them because of their inappropriate placing, but their position in **Z** is quite satisfactory.

(5) **Z** ıv 62-63: **Z** here shares what appears to be an impossible reading with the majority of **A** manuscripts (**A** ıv 61). The line probably contains some special phrase from the game of "handy-dandy."

(6) **Z** v 91 "Enuye ant Yre ayther wep faste": this line (discussed above, on the expansion of the confession scenes) contains Wrath, missing from **A**. The sequence of expansion proposed above removes the necessity for Manly's "lost-leaf" hypothesis.[59]

(7) **Z** vıı 5: here **Z** has a complete line, which it shares with **B** and **C** and **A** manuscripts EAMH[3] (textually related). **Z**'s support indicates that the line is genuine and that the loss of the second half must have taken place in the ancestor of the other **A** manuscripts (TChH[2] have what is clearly a filler).

(8) **Z** vıı 60 (**A** vıı 60): **Z** and **B** both have *lese*, a reading which Kane approves but does not adopt into **A** because of lack of manuscript authority. Clearly the archetype of **A** was at fault here.

3. Summary

Our explanation of **Z**'s peculiarities, then, is as follows: **Z** is (in restored form) Langland's partial revision of his first draft of the poem.[60] In the **A**-revision many of the weaker, repetitive lines were cut; some longer passages were eliminated; some parts were expanded (causing the temporary loss of Wrath, restored in **B**) and some passages were added.

---

[59] J. M. Manly, "The Lost Leaf of *Piers the Plowman*," *Modern Philology* 3 (1906) 359-366; Manly's hypothesis has been opposed by many scholars, e.g., George Kane, *Piers Plowman: the Evidence for Authorship* (London, 1965), pp. 17-18.

[60] See above, pp. 13-14.

The expansions often correspond to places where both **B** and **C** have further expansions. In the A-revision, **Z**'s minor inconsistencies were removed, and the Passus divisions were changed.

E. DATE OF THE **Z** VERSION

The allusions used to date the **A**-text (the Normandy campaign of 1359 and the south-west wind on Saturday, 1362) are both in **Z** (III 127 ff., v 32). **Z** lacks any later allusions, such as **B**'s episode of "Belling the Cat." The mention of Rome-runners in **A** IV 111 (**Z** IV 113) has been taken to imply that the Papal curia had now returned from Avignon to Rome (i.e., after 1367);[61] **Z** (Pr 57) says that "religious ran to Rome" to seek benefices. Neither reference, however, affects the date, as the curia was known as "Rome" whether the Pope was in Rome or not.[62] The phrase "all the wrights at Windsor" (**Z** VI 77) refers to the extensive rebuilding at Windsor, which was at its height in 1365 (see note), but building there continued throughout the century. In short, there is no way of dating **Z** any more accurately than of dating **A**.

F. TEXTUAL RELATIONSHIPS

This section is not intended to support our argument that **Z** is anterior to **A** but simply to present, as a corollary to our hypothesis, the relationship of **Z** to the other versions of the poem and to the several traditions of the A-version. Our hypothesis that **Z** (or, to be precise, the exemplar from which Bodley 851 was copied) is anterior to **A** both complicates and simplifies the textual history of **A**, **B**, and **C**. The problems it poses are exactly analogous to those affecting the relationship of **A**, **B**, and **C** themselves: just as there are some agreements of **AB** vs. **C**, **A** vs. **BC**, and **AC** vs. **B**, so we now have **ZA** vs. **BC**, **ZB** vs. **AC**, and **ZC** vs. **AB** (and also **ZAB** vs. **C**, **ZAC** vs. **B**, **ZBC** vs. **A** and **ABC** vs. **Z**).

---

[61] J. A. W. Bennett, "The Date of the A-Text of *Piers Plowman*," *Publications of the Modern Language Association of America* 58 (1943) 566-572.

[62] The concept "Ubi papa ibi Roma" (H. Walther, *Proverbia sententiaeque latinitatis medii aevi* [Göttingen, 1967], No. 32062e) is a commonplace of canon law. See Ernst H. Kantorowicz, *The King's Two Bodies* (Princeton, 1957), pp. 204-5; Michael Wilks, *The Problem of Sovereignty in the Later Middle Ages* (Cambridge, 1963), pp. 402-405. We owe these references to Dr. J. Tarrant.

1. Z in Agreement with B or C against A

There is, of course, no difficulty where **Z** has a reading not shared by **ABC**: **Z** is the earliest, and therefore the rejected, version. Similarly, **ZA** vs. **BC**, and **ZAB** vs. **C** simply show the stages in the poem's genesis.[63] The problems arise (just as they do in agreements of **AC** vs. **B**) when a **Z** reading persists in either **B** or **C** (or both) against **A**. These agreements are as follows:[64]

(1) ZB vs. A or AC

Pr 90	(= **B** Pr 223): *not in* **AC**
I 42	trangressores **ZB**: trespassours **AC**
II 16	**ZB** *agree: line differs in* **A** (**A** II 12)
II 125	sire **ZB**: *om.* **A**
II 148	*similar to* **B** II 174: *om.* **A** (**C**)
II 188-189	*similar to* **B** II 209: *om.* **A**
III 87	habbe **ZB**: holde **AC**
IV 20	stronge wytty **Z**, witty wordes **B**: wytful **A**
V 10	ye bydde **ZB**: it be þat **A**
V 52	here wastyng **ZB**: þat he wastide **A**
V 104	*similar to* **B** V 379: *om.* **A**
VII 152	to mysdon hym eftsones **Z**: if þei mette eftsoone **B**: whanne hy next metten **A**
VII 252	afyngred **ZB**: alonget **A**
VII 259	for lyflode ys swete **ZB**: lest liflode hym faile **AC**
VII 310	in borw ys to **ZB** (2 **B** *MSS differ*): breuesteris **A**
VIII 26	that they scholde **ZB**: And bad hem **AC**

(2) ZBC vs. A

Pr 96	castel **ZBC**: clyf **A**
Pr 129	seuth "*sees*" **ZBC**: shendiþ **A** (*see note*)
II 67	prynses of pruyde **ZBC**: present in pride **A**
II 70-71	in **ZBC**: *om.* **A**
II 85	Cyuyles leue **ZBC**: signes of notaries **A**

---

[63] This conclusion assumes that the readings of **BC** and of **C** are genuinely authorial and not the result of corruption in the archetypes.

[64] As noted above, "**B**" means the agreed reading of the **B** MSS (excluding idiosyncratic variants irrelevant in this context), not necessarily the reading adopted by Kane-Donaldson. "**A**" means all **A** MSS other than those cited with the lemma. The list does not include cases where some MSS of **A** have **B** or **C** lines in common with **Z**: these are treated separately below, pp. 23-24.

III 18   *similar to* **B** III 18 (**C** IV 19): *om.* **A**
III 115   gabbe **ZBC**: lie **A**
VII 3   of Rome **ZBC**: þe apostel **A**
VII 84   dowtres **ZBC**: frendis **A**
VII 136   to wrathen hym **ZBC**: arise **A**
VII 160   guttus **ZBC**: mawis **A**
VII 314   other bake (etc.) **ZBC**: *om.* **A**
VIII 13   yblessed that **ZBC**: þat blissen **A**

(3) **ZC** *vs.* **AB**

Pr 35   = **C** I 36: *om.* **AB**
(Pr 5 *similar to* **C** I 5: *om.* **AB**, *except* MS K, *which is contaminated by* **C**)
VIII 139   pyuysche **ZC**: pilide (pyned MH[3]) **A**, forpynede **B**
VII 202   herke **ZC**: here **AB**
VII 227   hym licuth **ZC**: nede is **AB**

These agreements can most simply be explained by accepting the Kane-Donaldson hypothesis that the archetype of the extant manuscripts of **A** and **B** were corrupt.[65] Thus, **Z** support for a line or reading would guarantee its genuineness. At the same time we must (*pace* Kane-Donaldson) allow that Langland may have changed his mind more than once (for example, by rejecting a reading during his **A** revision but reincorporating it in **B**). Also, Langland may have had access to several versions of the poem during his revisions. If, for example, he had one copy of **Z**, another of **A**, and another of **B**, it would not be surprising that readings of each persist, in a pattern now totally irrecoverable; also, Dr. Anne Hudson has suggested to us that Langland's own copy of the poem may have been corrected over a considerable period of time, incorporating his various revisions but without clear indication of which was the "correct" reading. Above all, of course, Langland must have worked from memory: recollection of a phrase from his earliest version could easily have slipped into the revision process at any time.

2. **Z** AND THE MANUSCRIPTS OF THE **A**-TEXT

The **A**-text is preserved in seventeen manuscripts (not all of which are complete throughout the Prologue and Passus I-VIII). Kane lists all the possible genetic families of manuscripts, together with their peculiar

---

[65] On the faulty archetype of the **A**-text, see Kane-Donaldson, **B**-text, pp. 75 note 15, 83, 205, 210-211 and note 172; for the archetype of **B**, ibid. pp. 70-97; for the hypothesis that the **C** revision was based on a deficient **B** MS (close to the archetype), ibid. pp. 98-127.

readings: the extensive cross-cutting between groups and the difficulty of establishing clear errors make it impossible to be absolutely certain about the genetic relationships.[66] This is not the time – nor do we have the space – to explore the effects that our hypothesis (of **Z**'s priority) has on the classification of manuscripts of **A**. We offer only a sample of readings to illustrate **Z**'s relationship with **A** manuscripts.

On at least one occasion **Z** is in disjunctive agreement separately with each of twelve manuscripts of **A**. It also agrees disjunctively with several of the groups of manuscripts discussed and described by Kane; on the other hand, **Z**'s agreements with these groups are minimal in comparison with their distinctive readings (even setting aside the large number of trivial agreements, such as omission of *and*, listed by Kane). This is a sample list only, and is confined to major lexical agreements; for convenience it is arranged according to the putative families discussed by Kane (devolving from the largest number to single members of the group); **Z**'s reading is given as lemma:[67]

(1) *EAMH³* [68]

VI 79-80 **ZEAMH³** (+ **BC**): *om*. **A** (*note that* EAMH³ *apparently have a third line, perhaps* = **B** v 594, **C** VIII 242). VII 5 ant ysowed hit aftur **ZEAMH³** (+ **BC**): so me god helpe TChH², *om. al.* v 163 syse **ZAM** (EH³ *differ*) (+ **C**): synay **A** (*most* **B**). VII 15 comawndeth **ZMH³** (EA biddeþ): wile (*etc.*) **A**.

VII 81 masse **ZAMH³** (+ **BC**): mynde **A**. VII 165 furst the fycyan **ZAMH³**: þe fisician ferst **A** (*see note*).

II 155 men **ZEAM** (some **B, C**): mene **A**. IV 32 aye **ZEAM** (+ **B**): into **A**.

VI 58 in no manere elles **ZEMH³** (+ **BC**): loke þat þou leiȝe nouȝt **A**.

I 92 tene **ZAM** (+ **C**): pyne **AB**. IV 151 mekenesse **ZAM** (+ **BC**): resoun **A**. II 12: *see note*.

VII 60 haue leue **ZMH³** (+ **BC**): haue **A** (*see note*). VIII 84 leden **ZMH³**: lyuen **A**. v 124: *see note*.

II 56 sesed **ZEM**: feffid **A**. II 130 togydderes **ZEM**: for euere **A**. III 93 hem the gate **ZEM**: þe treuþe **A**.

---

[66] Kane, A-text, pp. 53-114, summarized on pp. 112-114.

[67] As noted above, minor idiosyncratic variants are not taken into account; "A" means MSS other than those listed with the lemma. For a fuller account of Z's agreements with specific **A** MSS, see Charlotte Brewer, "A Study of MS Bodley 851," M.A. thesis (Toronto, 1979).

[68] Note that H³ is present only from v 102 to VIII 117 ; E lacks VII 45-62 and VII 212b ff., and A lacks Pr 1–I 90, II 22-154, III 61-176, VII 34-80, VIII 32-84.

I 54 mene mayne **ZM**: meyne **A**. II 94 **ZM** (+ **B**): *see Table and note*. II
      115 togydderes **ZM**: *om.* **A**. II 133 bad hem **ZM** (+ **B**): *om.* **A**.
      VIII 62 lye yc now trow ye **ZM**: ȝe wyten ȝif I leiȝe **A**.
VII 125 koes **ZA**: crowes/gees **A**.
VI 1 furst **ZH³**: faire **A**.

   (2) *WN*

IV 126 seyden **ZWN**: reherside **A**. III 32-33 (**C** IV 33, 32) **ZWN**: *om.* **A**.
I 24 courbed **ZW** (+ **B**): knelide **A**. III 22 coppus **ZW** (+ **BC**): pecis **A**. IV
      62 faste **ZW**: hym to helpe **A**. VII 95-96 faste ... yerne **ZW**
      (+ **B**): ȝerne ... faste **A**.
VII 132 aftur **ZN**: til on þe morwe **A**. VII 299 myd **ZN**: þerewiþ **A**.

   (3) *VH*

VII 26 petur **ZVH**: poule **A**.
I 22 lasted **ZH**: duriþ **A**. V 152 mysdedes **ZH**: wykkide dedis **A**.
VII 75 telleth **ZV** (some **B**, **C**): techiþ **A**.

   (4) *Other groups*

III 82 syxe **ZJLKWN** (+ **BC**): seue **A**.
VII 125 cach **ZAKNMH³**: chase/gaste **A**.
VII 165 yfet **ZWK**: defendite **A**.
III 86 prouendreth **ZKWNM** (+ **BC**): prouendrours **A**.
IV 17-18 (**B** IV 17-18, **C** V 18-19) **ZEAWM**: *om.* **A**.
V 75 **ZEKWM** (cf. **BC**): *om.* **A**.
IV 5 rather **ZEAWNM** (+ **BC**): erst (*etc.*) **A**.
VII 148 welde **ZRUDEA**: bere **A**.
II 187 dyne **ZJVL** (+ **C**): dome **A** (+ **B**).
V 59-60 (**B** V 32-33, **C** VI 135-136) **ZJEAM**: *om.* **A**.
I 86 plente **ZREKM** (+ **B**): plante (*etc.*) **A**.
VIII 41 graythe **ZTDChH²LKWN**: grete **A**.

   (5) *Other single manuscripts*

VII 317 gruche **ZR**: chide **A**.
V 55 Thomme Stoue **ZJ** (+ **BC**): Thomas **A**. (*For agreements of* J *with* Q,
      see notes to VIII 93 ff.).
VII 214 god **ZU**: þe **A**. (*On* QU *also, see* VIII 93 ff.).
Pr 5 (cf. **C** I 5) **ZK**: *om.* **A**.
II 194 schoppe **ZD**: shoppis **A**.[69]

---

[69] Variants as minor as this (sg./pl.) have not normally been noted: this is cited simply
to provide an example of agreement with D.

These data can be interpreted variously. As none of the **Z** readings above is a manifest error, the simplest solution would be to infer that as **Z** is the earliest version of the poem its support guarantees the authority of a reading. Often the reading of **Z** supports a reading preferred by Kane as the *difficilior lectio* or as the one most likely to cause corruption.[70] Sometimes **Z** agrees with the reading rejected by Kane.[71] It would be simple to argue that in the former cases Kane is right, and that in the latter cases he is wrong. For example, the **B/C** lines preserved in some **A** manuscripts, with **Z**'s support, may be original and have been omitted in error by the other **A** manuscripts; their retention in some manuscripts may indicate that these manuscripts represent the tradition faithfully, or that they have been independently restored from **B** or **C**. Independent conflation with **B** or **C** is very probable: WN and K, for example, have a great number of **C** lines which are not in **A** or **Z**.[72] In any case, the assumption that readings shared with **Z** are original and genuine involves no more problems with the textual history of **A** than exist already through convergent variation and cross-cutting between apparently genetically related groups of manuscripts.

On the other hand, the solution may well be more complicated. **Z**'s readings are, for example, well preserved in the EAMH³ group (especially MH³, despite the fact that H³ starts so late) and to a lesser extent in WN; only rarely does it agree disjunctively with the TRUDChH² group. The **A**-text may have gone through more than one revision, so that readings preferred by Kane but not supported by **Z** may represent a later revision. Such speculations, however, are beyond the scope of this Introduction.[73]

---

[70] Pr 15, 59, 109, 127, 137; I 6, 52, 97; II 35, 44, 90, 153, 156, 175; III 6, 46; IV 48, 65, 93; V 27, 64, 65, 137; VI 10, 29, 34, 42, 54, 55, 93, 96; VII 60, 94, 120, 185, 233, 279, 302; VIII 41, 108 (Q); cf. also I 105.

[71] Pr 39, 66, 129; I 53, 71, 109; II 39, 102, 139, 153, 175, 187; III 13, 42; IV 14, 106, 115, 135; V 13, 114; VII 5, 36, 176, 222, 311; VIII 30, 79, 106 (Q), 127 (Q), 140 (Q). This list (and the one in note 70) includes only those readings discussed by Kane in his Commentary or Introduction.

[72] On WN and K, see Kane, **A**-text, pp. 31-37.

[73] The hypothesis of authorial **A**-text revisions is perhaps supported by an examination of **B** contamination in **A** MSS relative to **A** contamination in **B** MSS. The former is very extensive (particularly in the EAMH³ and related **A** ms groups), while the latter is slight by comparison. One would expect the reverse to be true, since there were presumably more **A** MSS around at the time of the writing of **B** MSS than vice versa. Most of the **B** contamination in **A** MSS is shared by **Z**, which independently contains many more **B** readings. This strange situation seems best explained by the hypothesis of **Z**'s priority to **A** and **B** and the existence of more than one **A** version. Some **Z** readings were preserved in an earlier **A** version, eliminated in a subsequent **A** revision (i.e., those MSS that we now regard as characteristically **A**), and then put back in the **B** version. That is, the "**B** contamination" in **Z** and some of the **A** MSS need not be contamination at all,

G. LANGUAGE

A fuller account of the language of **Z** is provided in the Appendix (pp. 115-127); this present section summarizes the linguistic data that have a bearing on the nature of the **Z** version.

Words, lines and passages peculiar to **Z** show no linguistic differences from those shared with the **A**-text; that is, there are no signs of patching such as might be found if the scribe were interpolating passages into a deficient exemplar. For example, the "**Z** passages" contain the same mixture of East and West Midlands forms characteristic of the **Z**-text as a whole: superl. -*okest*, pres. 3 sg. in both -*eth* and -*es*, pres. 3 pl. in -*es*, -*eth*, -*e(n)*, both rounded and unrounded -*old*/-*ald*, *o* and *oe* for both /ǫ/ and /ǭ/, both *u* and *i*/*y* for OE *y*, *ui*/*uy* for OE *ȳ*, both *ch*- and *k*- in *church* according to alliterative needs, etc. There are no linguistic features that distinguish the "**Z**-passages" from the rest of the text.

As noted, the morphology and orthography of **Z** point to a dialect mixture of West and East Midlands. In addition to the features listed above, note the alternation of *sche-he-a* for "she" and *yow-ow* for "you." Admittedly, at this date no scribal language is ever dialectally "pure," but the evidence assembled in the Appendix points to a Western original copied by an Eastern scribe rather than to a scribe with a peculiar spelling system. If this is so, the hypothesis of a "memorial reconstruction" becomes less probable: one would expect someone writing from memory to write in a relatively pure dialect.

The hypothesis of a patched-up deficient exemplar or of a memorial reconstruction may, of course, be saved by supposing that the patching-up or memorial reconstruction took place in an earlier, Western copy, later copied into an East Midland dialect (i.e., in Bodley 851). The linguistic argument, however, is not confined to spelling and morphology. The vocabulary of the words, phrases and passages peculiar to **Z** is remarkably similar to that of the **A**, **B** and **C**-texts, not just in ordinary poetic words but in rare and apparently archaic words, some Western. An imitator might well deck out his "bridge-passages" with Langland-like words such

---

but instances of early authorial readings removed by Langland from the **A** tradition witnessed by TRUDChH[2] (the tradition normally preferred by Kane).

If this hypothesis is correct, there are substantial implications for the Kane-Donaldson **B**-text. Many **B** readings differing from **A**, rejected by Kane-Donaldson as corruptions in the **B** archetype, are found in both **Z** and one or more **A** MSS; if our hypothesis is correct, these readings may well be original and authorial. For a more detailed study of this point, see Charlotte Brewer, "*Piers Plowman*: Textual Implications of the **Z**-Version" (forthcoming).

as *ac, myd, weye, buyrne, freke,* and *gome,* and might, after a thorough reading of Langland, produce *bakken* "clothe oneself" (III 160), *harneys to pyke* "rob" (VII 67), *cammokes* "rest-harrow" (VII 91), *pulte* "pushed" (VII 182), or *neyghled* "approached" (VII 303). Would he, however, have included words such as *feym* "hunger" (VII 326), *faytles* "without deeds" (II 102), *stuty* "hesitant" (IV 124), *bewsoun* "fine fellows" (III 158), *wit* "drive away" (VII 59), *ourf-fors* "ox-tracks" (VII 64), *totraye* "torment" (V 113), *tyleth* "extends" (VI 66), *steme* "halt" (VI 75), or the West-Midland *botte* "bat" (VII 162)? Our experience of stylistic imitation at this period is limited, but Lydgate's *Prologue* to the *Siege of Thebes* or the alliterative satire *Mum and the Sothsegger* are relatively crude; Chaucer's *Sir Thopas* and his use of dialect in the *Reeve's Tale* are, perhaps, exceptions. If the **Z** passages are the result of deliberate imitation of Langland, their author must be credited with a very sophisticated linguistic sense.

The simplest and most economical explanation of **Z**'s linguistic features is that the **Z** passages are original (i.e., by the same author as the passages shared with **A**), that the whole of **Z** was originally written in a West-Midland dialect, and that this text was partially "translated" into an East-Midland dialect by a scribe of East-Midland origin (i.e., by John Wells of Ramsey and Oxford, into MS Bodley 851). The original exemplar from which he was copying had an orthography, morphology, vocabulary and syntax very close to what we generally recognize (from the **A**, **B** and **C**-texts) as Langlandian.

H. THE Q-CONCLUSION

The section written by hand *X* (probably John Wells) breaks off at **Z** VIII 92 (= **A** VIII 88); the remainder of the Passus (93-189 = **A** VIII 89-184) is written by a fifteenth-century hand, *Q*, who added a rhyming couplet and a colophon: *Explicit Vita et Visio Petri Plowman.* The end of Passus VIII occurs at the foot of fol. 140v, the first leaf of the new series of quires.[74] On fol. 141r *Q* began to write out the entire *Dowel, Dobet* and *Dobest* poem, ending on fol. 208r: *Explicit passus secundus de Dobest.* This latter part (fols. 141r-208r) corresponds to **C**-text Passus XI-XXIII, and is described by Skeat as "a very fair text" (of **C**). The end of Passus VIII is here referred to as section **Q¹** and the remainder as section **Q²**. The relationship of **Q¹** to **Z** is partly determined by an analysis of its language.

[74] See above, p. 3.

1. The Language of the Q-Sections

The purpose of this analysis is to discover the nature of the text from which Q took his texts of sections Q^1 (the end of Passus VIII) and Q^2 (*Dowel, Dobet, Dobest*) and its relationship, if any, to the exemplar from which **Z** (Prologue to VIII 92) was copied. For example, uniformity of language between Q^1 and Q^2 would tell us nothing about his source, as Q could consistently have altered the spelling of the original to conform to his own practices. As it happens, there is a marked difference between Q^1 and Q^2, particularly in the spelling of /*hw*/: in **Z** it is consistently *w*;[75] in Q^2 it is consistently *wh*; in Q^1, however, it is either *w* (*wan* 139, 154, 176, *wil* "while" 187) or *qw* (*qwan* 118, *qwat* 120, 179, *qweche* 155).

The orthographies of **Z** and section Q^1 are similar in other respects. Confusion between *ht*/*th*/*d*[76] is seen in the following: *rith* "right" 98, *ehte* "ate" 109, *fynth* "finds" 119 (*fynt* 117), *thynkyt* 120, *lettryth* "lettered" 101, *tawthe* "taught" 102, 189, pr. 2 sg. *mytist* 124, pr. 3 sg. *myth* 136. Such confusion is not a characteristic of section Q^2, which seems to keep -*th* (*þ*) distinct from -*ht* (-*ȝt*). Other Q^1 forms that resemble **Z** include: *wretyn* 98, *wyl* "well" 100, *say* "saw" 136, *lasse* 146, *schirche* "church" 160, *balder* 172, *thow* "though" 181, *deden* "did" 189; none of these appear to be features of Q^2.[77] Linguistic evidence, then, suggests that sections Q^1 and Q^2 were taken from different sources and that there is no evidence for a composite poem consisting of Prologue-Passus VIII *plus Dowel, Dobet and Dobest*; secondly, it suggests that Q^1 was copied by Q from the same exemplar as **Z**, with which it shares many features.

2. Section Q^1 and **Z**

Theoretically this section should be able to tell us where the **Z**-version originally ended, and thus where Langland ended his first draft of the poem. Unfortunately, the evidence can be interpreted in several ways. First, these textual features of section Q^1 should be noted: in VIII 93-189 there is a marked affinity with the **A** manuscripts J and U,[78] whereas **Z**

---

[75] See below (Consonants), p. 122.

[76] See below (Consonants), pp. 121-122.

[77] This is not the place to examine the language of section Q^2, which is the province of the editors of the C-text. It is, however, in some respects remarkably similar to that of **Z**: e.g., superlative *ryȝtfullokust*, inflexional -*us, seue* "seven," *gultus, murþe* (beside *merye*); the text from which Q copied *Dowel, Dobet* and *Dobest* may have been early and close to Langland's usage, just as (we have argued) **Z**'s was.

[78] Kane, *A-text*, pp. 8-9, 16; these two manuscripts have imperfect texts of Passus XII, otherwise found only in manuscript R (Kane, p. 51).

agreed with J or U no more than with any other single manuscript of the A-text; conversely, close agreement with manuscript M ceases in this section, and there are no agreements between Q^1 and the **B** and/or **C** texts such as were seen in **Z**.[79]

There are two principal alternatives: first that section Q^1 was derived from the same source as **Z**; second, that Q^1 was derived from a source other than the exemplar of **Z**. In favour of the first explanation are the linguistic arguments outlined above and economy – this latter explanation requires only two exemplars, one for ZQ^1 and one for Q^2. If we accept the first explanation we have to explain the unaccustomed textual affiliations of this section with manuscripts JU. It is possible that the exemplar from which **Z** was copied ended a quire at this point (VIII 92), and that the following gathering (containing at least the material in section Q^1) was lent out for copying, and thus became the source for JU. In support of this hypothesis is the fact that the section from VIII 93 to the end of Passus XII is almost exactly half the length of **Z** Pr 1–VIII 92: we could postulate three quires, of which the second ended at **Z** VIII 92 and the third contained the rest of the poem. Against this we must ask why Q stopped copying at the end of Passus VIII (the end of section Q^1) and turned to a **C**-text, but this query applies also to the second alternative.

In favour of the second explanation, that Q^1 is derived from a source other than that for **Z** Pr 1–VIII 92, is that it has the merit of explaining the Q^1JU affiliation and the absence of Q^1M and Q^1**BC** agreements: that is, Q^1 is no more than a copy of a bit of the **A**-text. If this interpretation is accepted, we must write off the linguistic evidence and the "draft" nature of VIII 113-114 (noting in passing that otherwise Q^1 does not have the other features that distinguish **Z** from **A**). We are left, then, to account for Q's change of exemplar for section Q^1 from the text that lies behind **Z** to one with a JU affiliation. This may have been because the exemplar was physically deficient at this point or unavailable to Q, or because Q for some other reason chose to ignore the exemplar of **Z**. There may, however, be a more interesting reason – that the **Z**-version itself, Langland's first draft of the poem, stopped at VIII 92. The validity of Truth's pardon remains unquestioned, and although the ending may seem inconclusive to readers who have the **A**, **B** and **C** versions in mind, the logic of the second vision is complete: Professor Burrow has pointed out to us that there is a close resemblance between the ending of **Z** at VIII 92 (where the old, weak, and sick that take their suffering meekly inherit the earth) and the

---

[79] See Charlotte Brewer, "A Study of MS Bodley 851," pp. 37 ff.

usual ending of the **A**-text at **A** xɪ 312 where the poor people "pierce with a Pater-noster the palace of heaven, Without penance at their departure into the High Bliss."

The literary grounds for preferring the second alternative are, then, very strong. Nevertheless, it is not inconceivable that **Z**'s exemplar continued beyond vɪɪɪ 92; we have therefore printed the remainder of the Passus, so that the reader may judge for himself.[80]

I. THE BODLEY 851 COPY OF THE Z-TEXT

1. *X*'s QUALITIES AS A SCRIBE

Textual errors show that Bodley 851 is simply a copy of the **Z** version, not the original. Three passages have been obelized; one (ɪ 101) probably shows a line still in draft form; two others may show some problem in the exemplar (probably lines that had been drafted and were not yet complete): v 124 *Quod ye nan*; vɪɪ 6 *ant schal*. Otherwise all errors are of a simple mechanical kind. Consequently the text has been presented with as little editorial tampering as possible, apart from the removal of blemishes that can be shown to be typical of *X*'s scribal habits.

(1) Literal errors: the scribe has corrected ɪɪ 96 *alle* (to *al*), ɪv 118 *auuanseth* (before *auaunseth*), v 116 *ger* (before *gret*), v 122 *alle* (to *ale*), v 132 *pw* (before *swythe*). We have corrected the following: ɪ 14 *women* (for *woman*), ɪ 51 *knigten* (for *knigted*), ɪɪ 50 *vn* (for *vp*), ɪɪɪ 8 *fo gyue* (for *forgyue*), ɪv 92 *me* (for *mede*), ɪv 108 *hteyn* (for *hetyn*), ɪv 141 *nllum* (for *nullum*), v 65 *th* (for *the*), v 72 *filij* (for *filio*), v 83 *one* (for *me*), v 118 *mada* (for *made*), vɪ 5 *sitteh* (for *sitteht* or *sitteth*), vɪ 32 *Pkyn* (for *Perkyn*), vɪ 40 *wost* (for *wolt*), vɪ 98 *woest* (for *worst*), vɪɪ 73 *tha* (for *that*), vɪɪ 148 *thay* (for *that*), vɪɪ 231 *ht* (for *hit*). Section Q[1] has similar errors but they are of a common kind: vɪɪɪ 130 *wordist* (for *wordis*), vɪɪɪ 139 *wyttens* (for *wyttnes*).

---

[80] A reader has suggested a third explanation to account for both the linguistic features of Q[1] (i.e., its similarity to **Z**) and the unusual textual affiliation of Q[1] with JU: namely, that originally Pr 1–vɪɪɪ 92 and vɪɪɪ 93-189 came from different sources, i.e., **Z** and an A-text of the JU group); that both sections were then copied by a West-Midland scribe into what was the exemplar for ᴍs Bodley 851, but with some indication of a break after vɪɪɪ 92; that scribe *X* respected this indication and stopped writing at vɪɪɪ 92 but scribe *Q* simply continued to the end of the Passus. This ingenious explanation "saves the phenomena" but is cumbersome. A further explanation might be that *Q*, while copying vɪɪɪ 93-189 from an exemplar close to JU, tried to imitate the spelling system already in use in the manuscript (i.e., in Pr 1–vɪɪɪ 92), but when he found a good **C**-text of *Dowel, Dobet* and *Dobest* he accepted its orthography and did not interfere with it.

(2) Confusion between *e* and *o*: these letters are easily confused in scripts of the period; it is not certain whether *X* was responsible for the errors or whether he was copying them. He himself corrects v 55 *Themme* (for *Thomme*). We have corrected: Pr 113 *reherso*, iv 149 *ronkus*, vi 3 *Bedlehom*, vi 13 *plowo man*, vi 81 *sethe* (for *sothe*). Where a form is acceptable we have left it alone, even though an error may have occurred: i 31 and v 73 *dome*, Pr 73 *wrochus* (see OED), v 32 *south-woste* (not recorded, but in weak stress).

(3) Confusion between *y* and *th*: iii 111 *the* (for *ye*), iv 132 *y* (for *þow*).

(4) Omissions: the scribe has supplied the following above the line: i 50 *ho*, ii 59 *here*, iv 121 *no*. We have supplied: Pr 84 *blyssed*, i 114 *kyn*, iv 112 *he*, iv 117 *yt*, iv 130 *thy*, iv 143 *on*, v 135 *the*, v 155 *none*, vi 37 *ye*, vi 38 *ye*, vii 35 *to my*. The following omissions are the result of haplography: i 81 *thow* (after *thow*), ii 117 *gyue* (after *gyle*), iv 32 *kyng tho* (after *the*), iv 88 *man that* (after *that*), v 135 *the*, vii 12 *yf* (after *yt*, or *yt* is an error for *yf*), v 135 *the* (after *bysowʒthe*); see note to v 135.

(5) Dittography: ii 168 whole phrase repeated from 164, iii 133 *thow pyte* written before *thow pylor*, vii 147 *ant ant* (for *ant*); see also vii 6 *the heye wey* (probably from 4).

(6) Apparent aural errors: ii 6 *boughtes* (for *bought vs*), iii 38 *of sentare* (for *ofsent hire*).[81]

(7) Anticipation of sense: the scribe corrects ii 93 *god* (before *trewthe*), ii 87 *Symonye* (corrected clumsily to *Cyuyle*), iii 141 *kyng* (before *lord*, perhaps anticipating 142), v 155 *there* (before *that*). We have corrected viii 91 *Ful* (for *For*).

(8) Incorrect line-division: this scribe (or another) has corrected v 128-129 by putting a stroke after *chestre*; at vii 265-266 the scribe wrote *may ... silf* at the end of 265, cancelled it, and wrote it correctly in 266; at vii 321 he cancelled *ne stryue* at the end and wrote it correctly in 322. We have corrected the following: Pr 60-61, i 90-91, i 95-96, ii 116-117, iii 133-134, v 63-65 (squeezed in at foot of page), v 165-166 (also at foot of page), vii 191-192. The division at vi 87-88 could be authorial; the division at i 79-80 could be a sign of the first draft version.

There are signs that *X* went back over what he had written: see i 96 *alle* corrected to *al* adv. He seems to have inserted initial *h* in many words, causing bunching of letters and the need for "separation marks": e.g., Pr 19 *hasket*, ii 95 *hast*, ii 98 *holy*, ii 123 *here*, ii 174 *hals*, iii 103 *han*, iv 63

---

[81] Such errors do not, of course, imply copying from dictation; see, for example, H. J. Chaytor, *From Script to Print* (1945; rpt. London, 1966), p. 19.

handi, etc. *X* may also be responsible for some of the punctuation that has been added (below).

2. LAY-OUT AND PUNCTUATION

The Prologue and each Passus except v begin with a decorated initial, red on a blue ground (in the style of Parts I and II of the manuscript); the initial *I* of Pr 1 is very elaborate. Passus v 1 begins with a simple majuscule *W* and capitulum mark. Each Passus (but not the Prologue) is headed in an Anglicana display script (e.g., *Passus Primus*).

Sections are marked off by a capitulum mark in the margin (preserved in this edition); this mark is also found at **Z** Pr 94 and **Z** v 155 (= **A** I 1, **A** VI 1), but not at **Z** v 19 (= **A** v 1). The capitulum mark is used inappropriately at II 183 (it would have been better at II 187), where the punctuator perhaps misunderstood *Symonye, sey hym* as "Simony saw him"; this probably shows that the capitulum marks were added later than the script. On the other hand, there is no evidence that the punctuator was using an **A**-text as the basis for paragraphing (otherwise he would have marked **Z** v 19); there is no correlation between the paragraphing and the passages peculiar to **Z**. At II 86 there is, in addition to a capitulum mark, a hand pointing to the line.

Lines are laid out as verse, except for the last two lines of Passus v, which are squeezed in at the foot of the page. Line endings do not always correspond to those of the **A**-text: most such divisions are probably errors.[82] Lines begin with small or capital letters, apparently indiscriminately. Capitals are rare, but *C* is often capitalized, even within the line.

The raised punctum is often used to set off small words such as *a, y,* and sometimes apparently just to space the letters. Bunched letters (especially where *h* has been inserted)[83] are separated by thin vertical strokes. Punctuation is effectively confined to Passus I-II; in I 1-95 the caesura and line-end are often punctuated with a punctus elevatus or a vertical stroke, often alternating, apparently according to a definite system of ictus or scansion. After I 95 only the vertical slash is used (at the caesura), except at II 59, 63, 64, 67, where the punctus elevatus is used. There is no punctuation after the end of Passus II. In four lines (I 80-83) the punctuator employs a curious symbol; two slanted strokes surmounted by a trefoil, first in an attempt to correct the wrong line-

[82] See above, p. 31.
[83] See above, p. 31.

division (by dividing after *louy*), in 81 and 83 to mark the caesura (after *synne, trewthe*), and incorrectly in 82 (after *wytnessett*).[84]

The punctus elevatus and the raised punctum were probably included at the time of writing the text; the capitulum marks, the vertical strokes, and perhaps the trefoil strokes, were probably added later. The identity of the scribe of the later punctuation can only be guessed, but as we have seen that *X* "proof-read" his text (e.g., by adding *h*) he may well have been responsible for the later punctuation.

J. THE PRESENT EDITION

1. SUMMARY OF THE ARGUMENTS

The arguments for the priority of **Z** have been presented seriatim throughout this Introduction and are here brought together. The differences from **A** in narrative sequence and in the presence or absence of lines and passages, and the occasional inconsistencies in the **Z** narrative, are best explained by assuming that **Z** is a revision of the earliest draft of *Piers Plowman* (or a copy of the earliest draft itself, with incorporated revisions); it includes strikingly Langlandian passages as well as many weak lines and readings which (both good and bad) are unlikely to be the result of scribal interference. Their character is such that it is simpler to find reasons why they would have been cancelled in revision than to explain their inclusion by a scribe. Textually **Z** sometimes agrees with **B** and/or **C** against **A**, and sometimes agrees with one or more **A** manuscripts against the others. **Z** presents a uniform linguistic appearance, close to a West-Midland exemplar with an East-Midland "overlay", of a kind unlikely to have been produced either by memorial reconstruction or by scribal editing. The probable date of the manuscript (ca. 1380) suggests that it was written not long after Langland's time of composition. At the same time, this is not a perfect copy: it can be restored by the elimination of minor scribal slips (of a type recognized by the scribe himself).

The main obstacle to acceptance of the priority of **Z** is likely to be the long-standing assumption that **A** is the earliest version – and, perhaps, some incredulity that **Z** could have remained unnoticed for so long. The latter is explained simply by the fact that **Z** is not an **A**, **B** or **C**-text and has therefore been ignored by editors of those versions. The best test of the hypothesis is the overall consistency of narrative sequence, style, and language; if the **Z** version is read without preconceptions of **A**, **B** and **C**, it

---

[84] On word-division, see below, p. 34.

will be found to present a poem so coherent (apart from the end of Passus
IV) that, if it had existed alone, its integrity would never have been
questioned.

2. Editorial Procedures

Emendation has been confined to the correction of simple errors:[85]
generally, the text has been preserved as it appears in the manuscript, even
where conjectural emendation would have been relatively easy (e.g., VII
6), on the grounds that this is a unique copy of a unique version of the
poem. To emend with reference to **A**, **B** or **C** would, in these circumstances, be likely to conceal evidence. Manuscript orthography has been
strictly preserved, but capitalization, word-division and punctuation are
editorial and follow modern practice. In the use of capitals, etc., we have
usually used Bennett's edition as a standard. All lines are given initial
capitals. The manuscript distinction between u/v is preserved, as is that
between i/j; where capitalized, however, *I* or *J* are printed according to
modern usage.

The scribe makes no distinction between *y* (= *þ*) and *y* (the vowel /i/ or
the palatal spirant); in this edition we have printed *þ* wherever it was
clearly intended (e.g., Pr 44 *þe puple*, passim 2nd sg. pronoun *þow*).[86]

The scribe frequently separates prefixes: e.g., Pr 7 *be fel*, 14 *by held*, 15
y maked, 33 *y thryueth*, 30 *a bowte*, 64 *there to, to gyderus*, 67 *vn lose*, etc.
Sometimes this results in ambiguity: e.g., Pr 58 *to a propre parsonages*
could mean "to have their own parsonages" or "to appropriate parsonages"; V 151 *to throngen* may be "then thronged" (*to = tho*) or
"thronged together" (from an unrecorded **to-thringen*); II 215 *bothe to
trembled* may mean "both then trembled" or "both two trembled" or may
involve an unrecorded verb **to-tremble* "tremble severely." Frequently
the pronoun *y* "I" is affixed to the verb (e.g., *fondy* Pr 18).[87] All word-
division in this edition is editorial: division such as *a tese, a nawnter* has
been altered, with a note in the commentary (but such cases have not been
treated as emendations). *Skynes*, as second element in *alle skynes, som
skynus* (VIII 34), has been treated as a separate word. Emendations are in
square brackets. Corrupt, unemended passages are marked by obeli.

Abbreviations are expanded and italicized in the text (except in Latin
words, which are themselves italicized). The following call for comment:

---

[85] See above, p. 30-31.
[86] See above, p. 31(3).
[87] See below, p. 115.

⁊ is used for the pl. and gen. sg. suffix and for pr. 3 sg.: when written out in full these appear variously as -*es*, -*ys*, and -*us* (e.g., Pr 5 *sellys*, 6 *hylles*, 2 *schrodus*). As the abbreviation is closer to ⁊ than to ꝑ, and is used in Latin *dignus* II 94, we have expanded it as -*us*.

ꝏ has been expanded -*ur*, even in words which usually have -*er* when written out in full (e.g., Pr 48 *aftur*); this treatment accounts for *Purnele* VII 279 (beside *Pernele* IV 104, V 53). Our justification is that ꝏ is the usual abbreviation for -*ur* (used, for example, in *purgatorye* II 75, etc.) and that -*er* is usually abbreviated ⟝, as in *water* Pr 10, *manere* Pr 19.

wᵗ has been expanded *wyth* (in full at Pr 23, etc.).

ꝫ̃ has been expanded *ant* (in full at Pr 5, 19, etc.).

qᵈ has been expanded *quad* (in full at III 56).

ꝑ has been expanded *per* or *par* according to modern usage, as the scribe seems to have intended both spellings (e.g., Pr 24 *parayled*, Pr 61 *parsche*, VII 104 *paradis*); thus, we have distinguished *parsones* Pr 61 from *persone* III 114.

ñ has been expanded to -*ne* in *vchone* II 111, II 203 (in full at Pr 108, etc.).

The bar through final ſſ has been expanded -*e*: at II 96 the scribe has corrected *alle* to *al*, apparently trying to maintain a distinction between the adjective and adverb.

The bar through final ꝉ has also been expanded to -*e* (VII 97, 109, VIII 92, etc.).

The curl on final rꝰ has been expanded (VII 17, 223).

Final ȝ occurs twice: at I 29 *yholdȝ* seems to be the pt. pp. *yholde*; at II 8 *standȝ* seems to be pr. 3 sg. *standet*.

Other final curls, on gꝑ and tꝑ, have been ignored.

3. AIDS FOR COMPARISON WITH A, B AND C

(a) *Text*

Words and lines in **Z** which are not in any manuscript of the **A**-text are printed in bold face, except as follows: if **Z** has two words, each of which is separately in some **A** manuscript, then the words are not in bold types unless sense or syntax is affected (e.g., VII 19); tense or number differences are not indicated in the text (but are mentioned in the Commentary). Whole lines which are shared with **B** or **C** and which are found in some **A** manuscripts (but rejected by Kane as the result of contamination) are in bold face: such **B** or **C** lines are noted in the Commentary. Differences of word-order from **A** and "omissions" of single words are indicated by a short vertical line in the margin; these are mentioned in the Commentary only if they are important (omission of *and* or pronouns is not usually mentioned).[88]

(b) *Concordance*

On each page the corresponding **A**-text line numbers are provided below the text; **Z** lines corresponding to **B** and/or **C** are indicated in the Commentary. Places where **Z** lacks a line or lines of the A-text are indicated in brackets, e.g., [om. **A** ...]. A full concordance of **A** and **Z** lines is given in the Table of Concordance, pp. 128-137.

(c) *Commentary*

As the "shape" of **Z** is essentially that of **A** Prologue and Passus I-VIII, the Commentary is designed principally to provide comparison with **A**, not with **B** or **C**. All significant differences between **Z** and **A** are noted, except for minor words (conjunctions, prepositions, pronouns, etc.) and morphological and orthographic/phonological variants. The sigla **A** and **B** normally refer to the consensus of all **A** or **B** manuscripts, except as follows. **B** and **C** (and individual manuscripts of **B**) are mentioned only when they agree with **Z** against **A**. As mentioned above, no signal is given in the text in cases where **Z** agrees with even one **A** manuscript; in the Commentary, however, agreement between **Z** and a single **A** manuscript is noted in brackets (in which case the siglum **A** refers to all **A** manuscripts except the one just mentioned), thus:

Pr 118   *lyueday* (J): *lyf days* **A** (I 27).

In the Q[1] section (from VIII 93) all agreements with **A** manuscripts are noted.

In readings of particular interest we have occasionally included mention of more than one **A** manuscript. In the citation of readings of **A**, the word "etc." means that other **A** manuscripts have readings which are either very similar to the one cited or are so different as to have no significance for **Z**. In the interests of economy of expression we have freely used expressions such as "some manuscripts," "most manuscripts": the reader would not be served by a repetition of material readily available in the editions of Kane and Kane-Donaldson. In the Commentary references are also given to Kane's discussions of specific readings, in his notes or Introduction. Our aim, in short, has been to facilitate comparison of **Z** with the A-text, and to provide **B** and **C** material and other information only where it is clearly germane to the textual status of **Z**.

---

[88] See above, p. 23.

William Langland

Piers Plowman

The Z Version

TEXT

Bold face words and lines are in the **Z**-text but not in the **A**-text. See the Introduction, p. 35.

Marginal vertical lines signal differences of word-order from **A** and "omissions" of single words. See the Introduction, p. 35.

Material marked with obeli (†) seems to be corrupt.

Supralinear words are enclosed in ` ´ marks.

RUNNING CONCORDANCE

Corresponding **A**-text lines are given for all **Z**-text lines.

Missing **A**-text lines are enclosed in brackets [*om.* A ...] at the appropriate place.

See also the Table of Concordance, pp. 128-137.

COMMENTARY

See the Introduction, p. 36.

Prologue

fol. 124r In a somer sesoun wen softe was the sonne
Y schope me into schrodus as Y a schep were,
In abite as an hermite vnholy of wer*cus*,
Wente wyde in this world wondres to here
5 **Ant sey many sellys, Y can nat sey alle.**
Ac in a May morwen **vnder** Maluerne hylles
Me befel a ferly, of fayre me thoughte.
I was wery of wandret ant wente me to reste
Vnder a brod **birch** by a born syde,
10 Ant as Y lay ant lened ant loked in the wat*er*
I slumbred in a slep, hyt sweyed so m*ur*ye.
Thone gan Y meten a merueylose sweue,
That Y was in a wyldernesse, wyst Y nere were.
As Y byheld in the est, an hey to the sonne,
15 Y sey a tour on a toft tryeliche ymaked,
A dep dale bynethe, **as dym as a cloude:**
Hit thondred, as me thou3te, th*er*e ant nawher elles.
A fayre feld ful of folk fond Y there bytwene,
Of alle man*er*e men, **bothe** mene ant ryche,
20 Werchyng ant wandryng as the world hasket.
Somme pote hem to plow, pleyuden ful selde,

Z 1-4 = **A** 1-4; **Z** 5; **Z** 6-21 = **A** 5-14 (15-16) 17-20.

5 Cf. K, **C** ı 5: *And sawe meny cellis and selcouthe thynges.*
9 *birch*: bank **A** (Pr 8).
15 *tryeliche*: supported by Kane (p. 163).
16-17 For these lines **A** (Pr 15-16 has):
   A dep dale beneþe, a dungeoun þereinne
   Wiþ depe dikes & derke & dredful of si3t
On the omission of the dungeon (see **Z** Pr 100), see Introduction, pp. 7 and 13.

21 *pleyuden*: the ms form could equally well be read *pleynden*, with good sense, but **A**,
B and **C** have some form of *play*. For the weak pret. suffix *-ud-*, cf. v 92.

| In settyng, in sowyng, swonken ful harde,
   Wonne*n* that wastres wyth glotenye dystruyen.
   Somme pote hem to pruide, *p*arayled hem thereaft*ur*,
25 In contynance, **in** clothyng, come*n* digised.
   In pryeres ant **in** pennaunses potte*n* hem monye;
   Al for loue of houre lord leuede*n* ful streyte,
   Al for hope to haue heue*n*riche blysse,
   As hankres ant h*er*myt*us* that holdeth hem in here sellys,
30 Coueyteth nat in cont*r*aye to kayren abowte,
   For no licorouse liflode here licam to plese.
| Ant su*m*me chosen chaffare, cheued the bettre,
   As hit semeth to oure syght that seche me*n* ythryueth.
   Ant su*m*me murth*us* to make as mynstrales conneth:
35 **Nolle noyth*ur* swynke ne swete, but swere grete oth*us***
   Ant as here licam loueth leueth thereaft*ur*.
   Byddares **as** beggares faste aboute yede
   Tyl here bagge ant here baly was bretful ycrammed,
   Faytede for here fode ant foughte*n* at the ale.
40 In glotonye, God wot, goth they to bedde
   Ant ryseth w*yth* ribaudye, tho Robard*us* knaues:
   Slep ant slewthe seueth hem eu*er*e.
¶ | Freres Y fond there of alle foure ordres,
   Preched þe puple for p*r*ofyt of the wombe,
45 Glosed the gospel as hem god lyked,
   For coueytise of kopys const*r*ued hit as they wolde.
   Hermytes on an hep w*yth* hoked staues
   Wente*n* to Walsingh*a*m ant here **wyues** af*t*ur.
   Pylegrymes ant palmeres plyhten hem togyderes
50| To seynt Jemes **of Gales** *ant* seynt*us* of Rome;

Z 22-34 = **A** 21-33; **Z** 35-36; [om. **A** 34-39]; **Z** 37-42 = **A** 40-45; **Z** 43-46 = **A** 55-58; [om. **A** 59-64]; **Z** 47-48 = **A** 50-51; [om. **A** 52-54]; **Z** 49-51 = **A** 46-48.

26   *pennaunses* (some **B** MSS, **C**): *penaunce* **A** (Pr 25).

35-36   35 = **C** 1 36; 36 is unique to **Z**. For this couplet **A** has Pr 34-39 (also in **B**, partly in **C**).

39   *faytede*: Kane (p. 160) prefers *flite* (Pr 42) as the *difficilior lectio*.

43   *I fond þere Freris* (etc.) **A** (Pr 55).

44   *preched* (most **B** MSS): *prechinge* **A** (Pr 56).

48   *wyues*: *wenchis* **A** (Pr 51).

50   *to*: *to seke* **A** (Pr 47).
     of Gales: om. **A**.

fol. 124v   Wenten forth on here way wyth many wyse tales,
            Ant haueden leue to lye al here lyf aftur.
            Bischopes blessed there beren here staues,
            Deden dygneliche here offices, Y deme hem neen other;
     55   **For tho apostles to prelatus apendeth here status,**
            Ant so Y leue they lyue ant lere vs the same.
            Religious to Rome ronne in a route,
            To apropre parsonages that pore clerkus hasketh.
            Barones ant borgeys ant bondage alse
     60   Y say in that semble, as ye schal here hereaftur.
            Parsones ant parsche prestus **preyd** here bischop,
            For here parsches were **so** pore sen the pestilence tyme,
            To haue a license ant a leue **to lauchen annueles**
            Ant take trentales thereto, to yer togyderus.
     65   **Seriauns serued there in selken houes,**
            Plededen for penyes ant poundes the lawe,
          | Ant for loue of oure lord vnlose here lyppe ones –
            Thow myghtest betur meten myst on Maluerne hilles
            Than geten a mom of here mouht or mony were yschewed.
     70   **Justices jugged that jeroures wolde schewe:**

Z 52 = **A** 49; **Z** 53-58; **Z** 59-60 = **A** 96-97; **Z** 61-63 = **A** 80-82; **Z** 64; [om. **A** 83]; **Z** 65 = **A**
84 + 85; **Z** 66-69 = **A** 86-89; [om. **A** 90-95]; **Z** 70.

53-58   Unique to **Z**.

55   Perhaps: "for those apostles – their rank pertains to bishops," i.e., apostolic rank
devolves on bishops.

57   See Introduction, p. 20.

58   For the sense, see MED *appropren* 1 (b).

59   *bondage*: supported by Kane (p. 434) for **A** Pr 96.

60   *hereaftur*: incorrectly placed at the beginning of 61 in **Z**.

61   *preyd*: *pleynide hem to* (etc.) **A** (Pr 80).

63-64   "To have permission and leave to receive (payments for) annuals and trentals as
well, two years together"; see MED *annuel* 2. Instead of these lines **A** has Pr 82-83.

65   Two lines in **A** (Pr 84-85).

66   *poundes*: this is the usual reading (**A** Pr 86), disputed by Kane (p. 434).

67   In **Z** this seems to be an incredulous aposiopesis: "But unloose their lips? — You
might as well measure mist...." All mss of **A** (Pr 87) have a negative, e.g., *Ac nouȝt, But
nouȝt, And nouȝt,* etc., attaching this line to the preceding one, which might be preferable
here. The syntax of **A** is also awkward.
     lippe (J, two **B** mss): *lyppes* **A** (Pr 87).

70-73   Unique to **Z**. That justices should feel bound by the decisions of juries is, in
modern terms, perfectly proper, but there seems to be a hint of the poet's disapproval.
Langland may have felt some dissatisfaction at the whole legal process: in the Middle Ages
juries had wide responsibilities and may have frequently been guilty of prejudice.

Were hit wel, were hit wrong, here word most stande.
Forthy lak y nat tho lord*us* – lawes they kepe
Ant saueth vs fro sorwes of synfol wroch*us*.

    | There preched a p*a*rdoner, as he prest were,

75   Ant broughte forth a bille w*yth* bischop*us* seles,

       Ant seyd that himsylf may soylen hem alle

       Of falsenesse, of fasting, of voues ybroken.

    | Lewed men leuen hym wel, liken ys word*us*,

       Comen vp knelyng to kyssen ys bulle;

80 | Bunged hem **on the hed,** blered here ey*us*

       Ant raughte w*yth* ys rageman ry*n*g*us* ant broch*us*.

       Thus ye gyuen youre gold glotonye to helpe,

       Ant leneth hit thys loseles that **in lecherie lybbyth.**

    | **Ac** were the bischop [blyssed] ant worth bothe eres,

85   Ys sel scholde nat be sent to deseyue the peple.

¶   Baksteres ant bocheres ant brewstres manye,

       Wollen webbestares ant weuares of lynnen,

       Taylours, towkares and tollares bothe,

       Myllares ant mynstrales and masones so*m*me,

90   **Of alle libbynge labores lopen forth there,**

       As dicares an delueres that doth here ded*us* ylle

       Ant dryueht forth the day w*yth* "Deux saue dame Emme!"

       Al this Y say **in my slep** ant seuene sithes more,

¶   **Ac the heye hyl in the Est, here wat hit menes:**

95   A louely laydy of lere in lynnen yclothed

Z 71-73; **Z** 74-85 = **A** 65-76; [om. **A** 77-79]; **Z** 86-89 = **A** 98-100 (101); **Z** 90; **Z** 91-92 = **A** 102-103; [om. **A** 104-108]; **Z** 93 = **A** 109; **Z** 94 = **A** ı 1 + 2; **Z** 95 = **A** ı 3.

78   *leuen: leuide/likede* (etc.) **A** (Pr 69).
     wordus (M): *speche* (etc.) **A**.

80   *bunged* (*bunchide,* etc. **A**): this spelling, presumably indicating /ndž/, is not recorded in OED or MED.
     on the hed: wiþ his breuet **A** (Pr 71). The A reading is stronger.

82   *glotonye* (V): *glotonis* **A** (Pr 73).

83   *in lecherie lybbyth: leccherie haunten* **A** (Pr 74). A's reading is stronger.

84   *blyssed:* om. **Z**, but needed for sense and metre.

89   Unique to **Z**: A here has Pr 101.

90   = **B** Pr 223.

92   *day* (M): *longe day* **A** (Pr 103).

93   *in my slep: slepyng* (etc.) **A** (Pr 109).

94   Unique to **Z**; A here has ı 1-2. **Z** has a capitulum mark beside the line: see Introduction, pp. 14-15, 32.

Com fro the **castel** ant calde me **twius**
  | Ant seyde, "Sone, slepest thow ? Sest this peple,
How besy they ben **the body for to plese**?
They an no ward to the hil that on hey standes,
100   **Ne no dred of the dongen in the depe dale."**

fol. 125r   Y was aferd of here face, thow he fayr were,
Ant seyde, "M*e*rcy, ma dame, wat ys this to mene?"
"The tour **wyth** the tofte," q*u*ad sche, "Trewthe ys therinne
Ant wolde that ye wroughten as ys word techeth,
105   For he ys fader of fayth ant formed yow alle,
Bothe w*yth* fel ant w*yth* flesch, ant yaf how fiue wyttes
To wyrschepe hym therew*yth* wyle ye ben here,
Ant therefor hygte the ereth to helpe you vchone
Of wollone, of lynne*n*, of lyflode at nede,
110   In mesurable man*e*re to make yow at ese,
Ant comaunded of ys cortesye in comewn thre thyng*us* –
Aren no nedeful but tho, ant nempne hem Y thenke
Ant rykene hem by resoun: rehers[e] ye hem aft*u*r!
That on ys vesture, fram chele the to saue,
115   Ant mete at **the** mele for myseyse of thysylf,
Ant drynke wen the druyeth, ac do nat out of resoun
That the worthe the wors wen thow wyrche scholdest.
For Loth in his lyueday, for lykying of drynk,
Dede by ys dowtres that the deuel lyked,
120   **For** lecherye hym lawghte, ant lay by hem bothe,
An al a wit hit the wyn that wyked dede.

Z 96-98 = **A** ɪ 4-6; [om. **A** ɪ 7-9]; **Z** 99-100; **Z** 101-119 = **A** ɪ 10-28; [om. **A** ɪ 29]; **Z** 120-121 = **A** ɪ 30-31.

96   *castel* (**BC**): *clyf* (etc.) **A** (ɪ 4).
    twius: faire **A**.
98   *the body for to plese: aboute þe mase* **A** (ɪ 6).
99-100   Unique to **Z**: "They have no regard to the hill that stands on high, nor any dread of the dungeon in the deep dale."
103   *wyth*: possibly a scribal slip. **A** (ɪ 12) has *on, in, of,* etc.
106   *how = ow* "you," a West-Midland form.
109   *of³*: supported by Kane (p. 434) against *to* in **A** ɪ 18.
113   *reherse: reherso* **Z**.
115   *Ant* (E, most **B** ᴍss): *þat oþer is* **A** (ɪ 24).
118   *lyueday* (J): *lyf days* **A** (ɪ 27).
119   After this line all **A** ᴍss except TChE (and all **B** ᴍss except C) have ɪ 29.

Dred dylitable drynke – thou schalt do the bettre –
Ant mesure his medicine, thow3 thow myche yerne.
| Hit ys nat al god to the gost that the guth hascuht,
125| Ne lyflode to the lycam that leue ys the soule.
Lef nat thy licam, for a lyare hym thecheth:
That his the wrechyd werld, wolde the bytraye,
For the fend ant thy flesch foleweth togyder*us*,
Ant that **seuth** thy soule ant seyth in thyn herte."
130 ¶ "A, ma dame, m*er*cy," q*ua*d Y, "me lecuth wel youre wordes.
Ac the money of thys molde that men so faste holdeth,
Telleth me to wam that tresor apendeth."
| "Go to the gospel that God sayde hymsylfe,
Tho the peple hym aposed w*yth* a peny in the temple
135 Were they scholde wyrschepe therew*yth* Cesar the kinge.
Ant God hasked of hem, 'Of wam spak þe letre
Ant ymage ylych that therein standes?'
'Sesaris,' they seyden, 'we seen wel vchone,'
'*Reddite Cesari*,'q*ua*d God, 'that *Cesari* byfalleth,
140 *Et que sunt Dei Deo*, or ye don ylle.'
For ryghtfoullyche Resoun scholde reule yow alle

Z 122-129 = **A** 32-39; [om. **A** i 40]; **Z** 130-141 = **A** i 41-52.

123   *his* "is."
127   *wolde*: supported by Kane (p. 434) on **A** i 37.
129   "And your soul sees that (i.e., the threat of World, Flesh and Devil) and speaks in your heart;" *seuth* = pres. 3 sg. *se-uth* (Appendix, p. 117). This interpretation (with *soul* as subject of the verb) is mentioned by Bennett (p. 106) for WO and is one which properly explains the **C** reading also (ii 39 *And that seeth the saule and seith hit the in herte*); Skeat took *Mesure* as subject. The **B**-text reads (i 41): *This and that seeþ (sees, seiþ, seest, sueth, sewe, s(l)eth) þi soule and (to* F, om. Y) *sett (setth, seith, saith, seeth) it* (om. OC²) *in þin herte.* **B** can similarly be interpreted "Your soul sees this and that (i.e., the several assaults of World, Flesh and Devil) and speaks it in your heart." Only the **A**-text varies from this sense (i 39): *And þat shendiþ (For to shende) þi soule set (and set, and seith* H²K, *& sent, see, I seo, take) in þin herte* (for the second half of the line EM have *be war of here wyles*). Thus, the **A** archetype must have had the error *shendiþ* for *seeþ*, which was variously accommodated by further alterations to the line (only H²K retaining the correct *and seith*). In **Z** perhaps read *yt* after *seyth* (omitted by haplography), as *say* never seems to be used meaning simply "speak."
    After this line all **A** MSS except RE have i 40.
133   **A** (i 44) has *quaþ heo* after *gospel*.
135   *were* "whether."
137   *ylych*: Kane (p. 434) argues in favour of the *y*-prefix.
138   *Sesaris* (M, most **B** MSS, **C**): *Cesar* **A** (i 49).

Ant Kynde Wyt be wardeyn, youre welthe to kepe,
Ant tutor of youre tresor to take hit yow at nede,
For hosebondry ant he holdeth togyderes:
145   **Trewthe techeth vs so to wyrche thereaft*ur*.**"

Z 142-144 = **A** ɪ 53-55; **Z** 145.

145   Unique to **Z**.

Passus Primus

           | I frayned here fayre, for hym that here made:
           "The dongen in the dale that dredful his of sygth,
           | Wat may hit mene, madame, Y beseche?"
fol. 125v   "That ys the kastel of care: ho so cometh thereinne
      5 May banne that he bore was to body or to soule.
          Thereinne wonyes a weye that Wrong ys hote
          Ant eke fad*ur* of falseed, **formed** hymsylf:
          Adam ant Eue he egged to ylle,
          Consayled Kaym to kylle*n* ys broth*ur*;
    10 Judas he byjaped w*yth* Jue*n* syluer
          Ant sennes on an hellerne hanged hym aft*ur*.
          He ys lettare of loue, lyeth hem alle:
          That trysteth on ys tresor, **trayed** as sone."
          Then haued Y wond*ur* in my wyt, wat wom[a]*n* he were
    15 That such wyse word*us* of holy wryt schewed,
          Ant halsened here on the heye name, hor he thenn*us* yede,
         | Wat **that** a were that wyssed me so fayre
          Bothe of falsenesse ant fayth: "Fayne nat, Y hote!"
          "Holy Chirche Y am," q*ua*d sche, "thow houghtest me to knowe.
    20 Y vnd*ur*fong the furst ant thy fayth taughte,
          Ant broughtest me borwes my byddyng to **holde,**

Z I 1-17 = **A** I 56-72; **Z** 18; **Z** 19-21 = **A** 73-75.

    6   *weye*: supported by Kane (p. 434) on **A** I 61.
    7   *formed*: *foundide* (etc.) **A** (I 62). Some **A** MSS agree with **Z** in omitting *it* before *hymsylf*.
   10   *of* has been incorrectly inserted above the line after *Juen*.
   13   *trayed* (*tyid* J, perhaps = *trayid*): *betraid* (etc.) **A** (I 68); cf. v 113 and note. Supply *is* (or emend *as* to *ys/is*).
   14   *woman*: *women* **Z**.
   17   *were*: *were witterly* **A** (I 72).
   18   Unique to **Z**.
   21   *holde*: *werche* (etc.) **A** (I 75).

| Wil thy lyf lasted to loue me **oure alle,**
    Ant eke to be buxum my byddying to wyrche."
| Thenne Y courbed on my knes, cryed here of here grace,
25 Preyed here petousely to prey for my synnes
    Ant **to** kenne me kyindely on Cryst to byleue,
    That Y myght werchyn ys wylle that wroght me to man.
    "Theche me to no tresor but telle me thys ylke,
    How Y may saue my soule that senne hard yholde."
30 ¶ "Wan alle tresores ar tryed, trewthe ys the beste.
    Y do hit on *Deus caritas* to dome the sothe:
    Hit ys as derworthe a drewerye as dere God hymsylf.
    For ho ys trewe of ys tonge ant telleth non other,
    Doth the wercus therewyth, wylneth no man ylle,
35 He ys a god be the gospel, a grounde ant alofte,
    Ant eke yleke to oure lord by seynt Leucus **lessoun.**
    Clercus that knoweth hit scholde kennen hit aboute,
    For cristene ant vncristene claymeth hit vchone.
    Euery wyght that ys wys wylneth hit to haue:
40 Kyngus ant knyghtus scholde kepen hyt be resoun,
| Ryden an rappe down in reumus aboute,
    Ant take **trangressores** ant teyen hem faste
    Tyl trewthe haued ytermyned here trespas to the ende.
    For Dauid in hys days dubbed knyghtes,
45 Dede hem swere on here swerd to serue trewth euere.

Z 22 = **A** 76; **Z** 23; **Z** 24-38 = **A** 77-91; **Z** 39; **Z** 40-45 = **A** 92-97.

22   *lasted* (H, *lestyth* one **B** MS): *duriþ* (etc.) **A** (ı 76); *lasted* may be pret. or pres. 3 sg.: see Appendix, p. 117. The word-order differs in **A**.
    oure alle: lelly (etc.) **A** (ı 76).

23   Unique to **Z**: partly repeats 21.

24   *courbed* (W, most **B** MSS): *knelide* **A** (ı 77) and **C**.
    of here (*on here* M): *of* **A**.

29   *that senne hard yholde* "who are held to be a saint" (*þat seint art yholden*, etc., **A** (ı 82)). For the spelling *senne,* cf. *sent* ıı 80, *seyn* v 69; *hard* shows inorganic *h* and *d/t* confusion (Appendix, pp. 121-123); the abbreviation in *yholdʒ* seems to be for *-e* (but see Introduction, p. 35). The scribe may, however, have taken *senne* as "sin" and *hard* as "firmly"; the scribe of D (*þat senne had yholden*) seems to have made this error.

31   *dome* (also at v 73): recorded as verb in MED, but in no **A** MS.

36   *lessoun: wordis* **A** (ı 89).

39   Unique to **Z**.

42   *trangressores* (**B**): *trespassours* **A** (ı 94) and **C**.

   | Þat ys profession that appendeth to knyghtus

Ant nat to faste a fryday in fifscore wyntur,

But halde wyth hym ant wyth here that haschet the trewthe

Ant neuer leue hem for loue ne for lachyng of yftus,

50   Ant `ho´ so passeth thys poynt ys apostata in the hordre.

   | Cryst, kynggen kyng, knigte[d] tene:

Cherubyn ant seraphyn, such seuene ant anothur,

Yaf hem mygthe in hys mageste – the murgur hym thoughte –

fol. 126r   Ant ouer ys mene mayne made hem arcangles;

55   Taughte hem thorw the trynite the trewthe to knowe,

To be buxum at ys **bede**, a bad hem nat ellus.

Lucifer wyth legyounes lerned hit in heuene

Ant was the louelokest of **lyght** after oure lord syluen,

Tyl he brak boxumnesse torw bost of hemsylfe.

60   Thenne fulle he wyth ys felawscipe ant fendes bycome,

Out of heue into helle hobeled they faste.

Somme in eyr, somme in herthe, somme in helle depe,

Ac Lucifer lowest lyth of hem alle:

For pruyde that hym **pulte** out ys peyne hath non ende,

65   **Ant apostata of that place ant pelour of helle.**

Ant alle that wyrcheth wyth Wrong, wenden they scollen

Aftur here deth day ant dwelle wyth that schrew.

Ac tho that wyrchen the word that holy wryt techeth

Ant endeth as Y or sayde in parfite **vertus,**

Z 46-64 = **A** 98-116; **Z** 65; **Z** 66-69 = **A** 117-120.

50 *ho*: inserted above the line.

51 *knigted: knigten* **Z**.

52 *such seuene ant anothur*: supported by Kane (p. 160) on **A** ı 104.

53 *hym*: Kane prints the majority reading *hem* (**A** ı 105), referring to the angels, but notes (pp. 154-155) that *hym* (DEM) offers a challenging alternative.

54 *mene mayne* (M, most **B** mss): *meyne* **A** (ı 106).

56 *bede: bidding (heste, bone)* **A** (ı 108).

58 *lyght* (some **B** mss): *siʒt* (etc.) **A** (ı 110).
  syluen (M): om. **A** (*dere* J).

61 *heue* "heaven."

64 *hym* (W, **C**) refers to Lucifer, object of *pulte* (cf. ms H of the **B**-text: *hem putte*); most **A** and **B** mss have *þat he put out*, etc. (**A** ı 116).

65 Unique to **Z**: cf. **Z** ı 50.

69 *vertus: werkis* **A** (ı 120).

70   Mow be syker that here soule schal wende to heuene
     There trewthe his in trinite, ant tronen hem alle.
| Forthy Y seyde er by syght of thys tyxtes:
     Wen alle tresores ar tryed, trewthe ys the beste.
¶   Lere hyt thus to lewed men, for lettred hyt knoweth,
75   That trewthe his the tresor trydest on erthe."
     "I haue no kynde knowyng: yut mot ye kene me betre
     By wat craft in my cors hyt comseth ant were."
     "Thow doted daffe," quad sche, "dulle are thy wyttes!
| Hyt ys a kynde knowyng that keneth
80   For to louy thy god leuere than thyselue;
     To do no dedly synne, deye thow [thow] scholdest,
     For thus wytnessett ys word: wyrche thow thereaftur!
     Thys, Y trowe, be trewthe; ho can theche the bettere,
     Loke thow suffre hym to seye ant senes lere hit aftur.
85   For loue his the leuest thynk that oure lord hasketh,
     Ant eke the plente of pes – preche hit in thyn harpe,
     There thow art murye at the mete, yf men byt the yed.
¶   For in kynde knowyng in herte there comseth a myght,
     Ant that falleth to the fadur that fourmed vs alle,
90| Loked on vs wyth loue, let ys sone deye
     Mylelyche for oure mysdedes to menden vs alle,
     Ant yut wolde hem no wo that wrowghte hym that tene,
     But mikelyche wyth mouthe mercy a bysowghte,
     To haue pite on the peple that peyned hym to dethe.

Z 70-81 = **A** 121-132; **Z** 82 = **A** 135; **Z** 83-84 = **A** 133-134; **Z** 85-94 = **A** 136-145.

71   *tronen*: Kane (p. 435) argues for *troniþ* (**A** ı 122), with Truth as subject.

72   *Forthy*: *Forþi I seye as* **A** (ı 123).

76   *I haue* (M, two **B** MSS, **C**): *ȝet haue I* **A** (ı 127).

79-80   Written as one long line, with a caesura mark after *louy* (see Introduction, p. 32). This may represent an early draft: "it is a natural knowledge that teaches (you) to love your God dearer than yourself"; when *in þin herte* was added in **A**, *for to louy* was taken into the next line. On the other hand, the scribe's line division is often incorrect (Introduction, p. 31), and *in thyn herte* may have been inadvertently omitted.

81   *thow*: om. **Z** (haplography).

82   After 84 in **A**.

86   *plente*: MSS of **A** and **B** vary between *plente* and *plante*; most editors (Skeat, Bennett) read *plante*, referring to Isa. 53:2. Kane also reads *plante*, but tentatively (p. 155) suggests *planete*. In support of *plente*, cf. Rom. 13:10 *plenitudo ergo legis est dilectio*.

91   *mylelyche*: placed at the end of 90 in **Z**.

95   Here myght thow se ensawmples in hymsylf one,
     That he was myghtfol ant meke ant mercy gan graunte
     To hem that hongen hym heye ant ys herte thorled.
     Forthy Y rede, ye ryche, habbeth rewth on the pore;
     Thow ye be myghty to mote, beth meke in youre wercus:
100 **Loketh on hem wyth loue-lawes, thow ye hem kepe.**
     †For the same mesures that methet amys†
     Other alles ye schal be wo therewyth wen ye wenden hennus.
     Thouȝ ye be trewe of yor tonge ant trewlyche wynne
     Ant be as schast as a childe **ant do chirches make,**
fol. 126v But yf ye loue lelelyche ant lene the pore,
106 Of such god as God ou sent godlyche parte,
     Ye habbeth no more meryte in masse ne in houres
     Then Maleken of here maydenhod that no man desyreth.
  | James the gentel iuggeth by ys bokes
110 That fayth wythouten the fet ys febler then nauȝt
  | Ant as ded as a dorenayl, but yf dedus folwe.
     Mony chapelyns aren chaste, ac charite ys aweye.
     Aren noen harder then **summe** wen they ben avaunsed,
     Ant eke vnkynde to here [kyn] ant to alle other crystene;

Z 95-99 = **A** 146-150; **Z** 100; **Z** 101-111 = **A** (151-152) 153-161; [om. **A** 162]; **Z** 112-
114 = **A** 164-166.

95   *one*: placed at the beginning of 96 in **Z**.

97   *heye*: supported by Kane (pp. 106, 435) at **A** ı 148 against *by*, which would refer to
the thieves crucified with Christ.

100 Unique to **Z**.

101-102   For these lines **A** (ı 151-152) has:
     For þe same mesour ȝe mete, amys oþer ellis,
     Ȝe shuln be weiȝe þerwiþ whanne ȝe wende hennes (etc.)
The **Z** version may be no more than a scribal slip, but it could represent the first draft of
the lines: 102 may follow directly from 100 and mean "or else you will be sorry for it,
when you go hence;" 101 would be parenthetic, a partial translation of *eadem mensura
qua mensi fueritis* (cf. **B** ı 178a). In the **A** revision the translation was completed, resulting
in the change from *wo* to *weiȝe* "weighed" and the moving of *other alles* to the preceding
line.

104 *ant do chirches make: þat in chirche wepiþ* **A** (ı 154). The **Z** version may have
been cancelled because of Meed's later offer (not in **Z**) to help the friars in church building
(**A** ııı 47 ff.).

109 *iuggeth*: Kane (p. 435) argues for *ioynide* (**A** ı 159).

112 ff.   The line order differs from that in **A** (ı 161 ff.), which uses the same line (**Z**
117) twice: see the concordance above and Table of Concordance.

113 *summe: hy/thay* (etc.) **A** (ı 165).

114 *kyn*: om. **Z**, but needed for sense and alliteration.

115   Cheweth here charite, chyde*n* aft*ur* more.
       Here loue ys likned to a lau*m*pe that no lyght ys ynne:
       Such chastite wyth*outen* charite worth cheyned in helle!
       For ye curatores that kepeth yow clene of youre body
       Ant beth acombred wyt*h* couetyse, ye konne*n* nat crepe out,
120   So harde haueth auarice yhapsed yow togyderes, –
       Trewthe taughte neue*r*e so, but trecherye of elle –
       Ant **lereth** the lewed men later to dele,
       Foryth word*us* ywryte in the ewangelye:
       '*Date et dabitur vobis,* for Y dele yow alle.'
125| That ys lok of loue that lateth out grace
       To conforte the carful acombred wyt*h* synne.
       Loue ys the **lyfloede** that oure lord haschet,
       Ant eke the **gate of grace** that goth into heune.
  | Forthy, seye as Y seyde er, by syght of this tyxt*us*:
130 Wen alle tresoures ben tryed, trewthe ys the best.
       Now haue Y told the wat trewthe ys – **taken in thyn herte.**
       Y may no leng*ur* lenge **the wyth** – now loke the oure lord!"

Z 115 = **A** 167; **Z** 116 = **A** 163; **Z** 117 = **A** 162 (= 168); **Z** 118-132 = **A** 169-183.

116   *Here loue ys likned to: It is as lewid as* **A** (ɪ 163). The **A** reading is more dramatic.

117   Quoted on fol. 3r among the flyleaf proverbs which were added in the fifteenth century, with *brennit* for *cheyned*. See "Medieval Latin Poetic Anthologies (II), *Mediaeval Studies* 40 (1978) 405, Appendix No. 54.
    cheyned: supported by Kane (p. 435) on **A** ɪ 162, 168.

121   *Trewthe taughte neuere so: þat is no treuþe of trinite* **A** (ɪ 172).

122   *lereth* (ʒe lere E): *lering/lernynge* (etc.) **A** (ɪ 173).

123   *Foryth* (*For yth*): *For þise arn þe* (etc.) **A** (ɪ 174). The spelling *foryth* "forgets" is explained by the loss of the initial palatal spirant (cf. *yf* "give," *yftus* "gifts") and inflexional *t/th* confusion (see Appendix, pp. 117, 122). The subject of *lereth* and *foryth* is *auarice* 120.

127   *lyfloede*: *leueste þing* **A** (ɪ 178). For the sense, see MED liflode (3(a).

128   *gate of grace*: *graiþ* (*gret, graciouse,* etc.) *gate* **A** (ɪ 179) and **B**: *graffe of grace* **C**.

129   *seye: I seiʒe* **A**. In **Z** the verb may be imperative, unless it is an error, but **A**'s reading is smoother.

131   *taken in thyn herte: þat no tresor is betre* **A**. Either "what truth is taken in your heart" (which makes little sense) or *taken* is an error for *take yt,* imperative.

Passus Secundus

Now haue Y told yow of trewthe, that no tresor ys bettre.
Yf ye wyl weten of Wrong, Y wyl yow fayre schewe
Bothe of Fauel ant Falsede that myche folk apeyreth.
For yut Y kneled on my knes ant cryed here of grace

5 Ant seyde, "Mercy, madame, for Marie loue of heune
That bar that blysful barn that bought [vs] on the rode!
| Kenne me **for youre cortesye** the False for to knowe."
"Loke on the lifth half," quad sche, "ant lo, were a standet,
Bothe Fauel ant False ant ys feres monye.

10 **Yf thow wylnes to wytte, lo, were they stande."**
I loked on my lifth half, as the lady me thaughte,
Ant was ware of a wuiman worthely yclothed,
Yporfyled **in** pelure, the purest on erthe,
Ycrowned in a crowne, the kyng hatht no bettre.

15 Alle here fyue fyngres were fretted wyth ryngus,
Wyth ryche rubius as rede as a glede,
In red scarlet yrobed ant **rybanes of** golde:
There ys no quene queyntor that quyk ys on **molde.**

Z II 1-3 (cf. **A** I 182); **Z** 4-9 = **A** II 1-6; **Z** 10; **Z** 11-15 = **A** 7-11; **Z** 16 (cf. **A** 12); **Z** 17-18 = **A** 13-14.

1-3 Unique to **Z**; presumably spoken by the poet rather than Holy Church or the dreamer, and cancelled in **A** because they are unnecessarily intrusive.

6 *bought vs: boughtes* **Z**, perhaps an aural error: see Introduction, p. 31.

7 *for youre cortesye: be sum craft* (etc.) **A** (II 4), with changed word order.

8 *standet: standʒ* in text: see Introduction, p. 35, Appendix, pp. 116-117 especially n. 5, and **Z** I 29.

9 *Fauel ant False* (one **B** MS): reversed in **A** (II 6).

10 Unique to **Z**: cf. **Z** II 8.

12 *worthely* (M, some **B** MSS): *wondirliche* (etc.) **A** (II 8). A-text MS A has *worthily* before *war*, but *fayre clothid.*

16 = **B** II 12 (cf. **C** III 13), quite different from **A** II 12.

17 *rybanes of* (**B**): *ribande wiþ* (etc.) **A** (II 13).

18 *molde* (*erthe* E): *lyue* **A** (II 14).

"Wat ys that wuima*n*," q*ua*d Y, "so worthyly atyred?"
20   That ys Mede the mayde," q*ua*d he, "hath nuyed me ful ofte
fol. 127r   Ant laked my lore to lord*us* aboute.
In the Pope paleys he ys pryue as mysylfe,
Ant so scholde sche nat be, for Wrong ys here syre.
Out of Wrong sche wax to wroth*ur*hele monye:
25   I howghte ben herrer than he, Y com a bettre.
Tomorwe worth the maryage mad of Mede *ant* of Fals:
Fauel w*yth* fayr speche hath forged hem togyderes,
Ant Gyle hath bygo here so, he graunthet alle h*er*e wylle,
Ac alle ys Lyares ledyng that they lye togyderes.
30   Tomorwe worth the maryage ymad, as Y telle:
There myght thow wytte, yf þou wylt, wyche they ben alle
That longeth to **thys** lordschipe, the lasse *ant* the more.
Knowe hem there, if thow canst, ant kepe the fro hem alle,
Yf thow wylnest to wone w*yth* Treweth in ys blisse.
35   Y may no lengor lette, lord Y the bykenne –
Ant bycome a god man, for eny couetyse, Y rede!"
Alle the ryche retenanse that regneht w*yth* False
Were bede to this bruydale on bothe to the sydes.
Sire Symonye ys ofsent to sele the chartres
40   **Ant alle the notaryes by name, that they noen fayle,**
To sette on here sygnes as Symonye wyl bydde.
Cyuyle ys sompned to sese alle the lond*us*
That Fauel ant Fals by eny fyn haldeth,
To feffe Mede theremyd in maryage for eu*ere*.
45   **Sothnesse ant myself sey this ant more,**

Z 19-39 = **A** 15-35; **Z** 40-42; **Z** 43-44 = **A** 36-37; **Z** 45.

19   First four words written out again at foot of page, by a later hand.
22   *Pope* (V): *Popes* **A** (ɪɪ 18); see Appendix, p. 116.
25   *a* "of."
28   *he* "she" (Meed). *here*² (M): *his* **A** (ɪɪ 24).
35   *lord*: supported by Kane (p. 435) on **A** ɪɪ 31.
38   *bothe to the sydes* (as in VL) "both sides" (*to* = "two"): *boþe two sides* **A** (ɪɪ 34).
39   *ofsent*: Kane (p. 435) argues in favour of *assent* in **A** (ɪɪ 35).
40-42   Unique to **Z**.
43   *Fauel ant Fals* (E): reversed in **A** (ɪɪ 36); cf. **Z** ɪɪ 9 above.
44   *theremyd*: supported by Kane (p. 157).
45   Unique to **Z**. On Soothness, see Introduction, p. 16.

For there nas hale ne hows to herborwe the peple,
Nayther logge ne lawnde ne lesewe so brode,
That vch feuld nas ful of folk alle aboute.
| In myddys on morwe on a montayne heye
50   Was pyght [vp] a pauel*i*on, proud for the nones,
An ten thowsound of tent*us* teled by sydes
Of knyght*us* of contrays ant commiers aboute,
For sysores, for sompnor*us*, for syllares ant bygares,
For lered, for lewed, for laboreres **in thowne** –
55   Alle to wyttenesse wel wat the wryt wolde,
In wat man*e*re that Mede in **meble** was sesed,
Ant to by fastened w*yth* Fals the fyn ys arered.
Thenne Fauel fecheth here forth ant to Fals taketh,
In forward that Falsede schal fynde `here´ for euer*e*
60   **Ant to be boun at ys bede at bord ant at bedde,**
As sire Symonye wyl segge, to sewen ys wylle.
| Symonye ant Cyuyle **thenne** standeth forth
Ant vnfoldeth the feffement that Fals hath ymaked.
Thus bygynneth thyse gomes ant gredeth ful heye:
65   "Wythet ant wytnesseth that wonyeth on erthe,
That Y, Fauel, feffe Falsnesse to Mede,
To be **prynses of** pruyde **in** pore ant **in** ryche,
W*yth* alle the lordchepe of lecherye a lengthe ant of brede,
Wyth the erldom of enuye for euere to laste,
70   **Ant alle the counte of couetyse yknowen aboute,**

Z 46 = **A** 38; **Z** 47; **Z** 48-59 = **A** 39-50; **Z** 60 = **A** 51 + 52; **Z** 61-67 = **A** 53-59; **Z** 68 = **A** 61; **Z** 69 = **A** 60; **Z** 70; [om. **A** 62-65].

47   Unique to **Z**: "neither lodge (tent) nor field (lawn) nor meadow so broad."

50   *vp: vn* **Z**.

54   *in thowne: of þropis* (etc.) **A** (II 45); *thowne* "town."

56   *in meble was sesed: in mariage was feffid/sesyd* (etc.) **A** (II 47). The **A** alteration was perhaps made because Meed's property from the settlement (68 ff.) was not chattels but real estate.

59   *here: sup. lin.*

60   Expanded into two lines in **A** (II 51-52).

62   *thenne:* om. **A** (II 54). *forth: forþ boþe* (etc.) **A**.

64   *ful* (J, most **B** MSS): *wel* **A** (II 56).

67   *prynses of pruyde* (**BC**): *present in pride* **A** (II 59).

69   Placed after 67 in **A**.

70-72   Replaced by **A** II 62-65, which uses some of the same vices (covetousness, usury and avarice) and adds great oaths and lust. For 70-71, compare **B** II 86-87, **C** III 90-

fol. 127v   **As in vsurye, in auaryse, in oth*ur* cheuysawnses,**
                Tyl that glotenye be ygraue here glorye to deure,
                W*yth* the seynewrye of slewethe Y sese hem togydere,
                They to habbe ant to holde, ant here herrys aft*ur*,
          75   W*yth* alle the portenaunce of p*ur*gatorie into the pyne of elle,
                Yelding for thys thyng at one yeres ende
                Here sowles to Satanas to synken in pyne,
                There to wonyen w*yth* Wrong, wyle God ys in heuene."
                In wyttnesse of wych thyng Wrong was the furste,
          80   Ant Peres the p*ar*doner **of Sent Poules chirche,**
                Ant Bette the bedel of Bokyngh*a*mschire,
                Ant Reynald the reue of Rotlonde sokene,
                Monde the myllare, ant mony mo oth*ur*.
                In the date of deul thys dede ys aseled
          85   By syght of syre Symonye ant **Cyuyles leue.**
          ¶   Thenne tened hym Theologye wen he thys tale yherde
                Ant seyde to [Cyuyle,] "Now sorwe on thy bokes,
                Such weddin*gus* to wyrche to wrathe*n* **the** trewthe,
                Ant ar thys wedding be wrought, wo the betyde!
          90   For Mede ys moylere of Mendes enge*n*dret:
                God grawnteth **hymsylf** to gyue Mede to Trewthe,
                Ant thow hast gyue here to a **gloten.** Now God gyue the sorwe!
                The tyxt*us* telleth nat so; Trewthe wot the sothe:
                ***Dignus est operarius* hys huyre to haue,**

Z 71-72; **Z** 73-93 = **A** 66-86; **Z** 94.

91. 72 has no parallel in **A**, **B** or **C**. The passage is further altered and expanded in the
revision from **A** to **B**.

   80   *of Sent Poules chirche: poulynes doctor* **A** (II 73). The word *Paulyne/Poulyne* has
caused problems for commentators: Bennett (on **B** II 108) suggested that it might refer to
St. Paul's or its neighbourhood, which is supported by the **Z** reading.

   85   *Cyuyles leue* (**BC**): *signes of notories* **A** (II 78); cf. **Z** II 40-41.

   87   *Cyuyle:* the scribe first wrote *Symonye,* and then altered the first four letters to
Cyuy, leaving the correction incomplete.

   88   *weddingus* (N, some **B** MSS): *weddyng* **A** (II 81).
      the: wiþ **A**. The definite article in **Z** suggests that Truth is not a character at this point.

   90   *Mendes:* supported by Kane (pp. 99, 436).

   92   *gloten: gilour* **A** (II 85). The **A** reading fits False better.

   93   *god* cancelled and expunged before *trewthe.*

   94   = **B** II 123; also in this form in **A**-text MS M. Otherwise the **A**-text (II 86a-87) gives
a full line to the Latin quotation and an expanded line of English:
          Dignus est operarius mercede (sua)
          Worþi is þe werkman his mede to haue
Two other **A** MSS (besides M) have "hire" for "meed": *hure* V, *huyre* H. In **A** *mede* does

95   Ant thow hast faste here w*yth* False, **we**! fy on the lawe!
      For al by lesyng*us* tow lyuest ant lechoures werc*us*.
      Thow schalt abygge **thys bargayn by my fad*ur* sowle!**
      Sire Symonye ant thysylue schendeth holy chirche,
      W*yth* notaryes nysotes nuyest the peple,
100   **Ant sowsest yow in synne w*yth* seynte Marye rent*us*.**
      Wel ye wyte, wernard*us*, but yf youre wyt fayle,
      That Fals hys a faytor ant faytles of werc*us*,
      Ant as a bastard ybore of Belsabubbes kynne,
      Ant Mede ys a **mayde, murgust on erthe –**
105   A myghte kysse the kyng for cosyn, ant he wolde.
      Ac wurcheth by wysdo*m* ant by wyt aft*ur*
  | Ant ledeth here to Londone there **lewte** hys handlet,
  | Yf eny **lawe** wyl loke they lygge togyderes.
      Ant thow iustises **iuggede** here to be ioyned w*yth* False,
110   Yut beth ywar of the wedding, for wytty hys Trewthe,

Z 95-96 = **A** 88-89; **Z** 97 (cf. **A** 92); **Z** 98-99 = **A** 90-91; **Z** 100; **Z** 101-110 = **A** 93-102.

not alliterate. Kane (p. 436; cf. p. 106) argues that no scribe would have substituted the unmetrical *mede* for *hire* (which provides *aa bb* alliteration) and therefore regards *mede* as the original reading. Presumably, according to Kane's interpretation, the readings of VH are the result of scribal substitution of an alliterating word, that of M results from contamination by **B**, and the **B**-text itself is either a revision or a line based on an inferior copy of the **A**-text. According to our hypothesis, the reading of **Z** (and M and the **B**-text) is the original (with vocalic alliteration on *operarius, huyre, haue*) and **A** the revision; VH would show the incomplete revision towards the **A** version of the line, and, as elsewhere, M and the **B**-text have the original, earliest version.

95   *we*: om. **A** (ɪɪ 88).

96   *al*: corrected in the ᴍs from *alle* (see Introduction, p. 30).

97   Compare **A** ɪɪ 92: *ʒe shuln abigge boþe, be god þat me made.* After 99 in **A**.

99   *wyth notaryes nysotes*: *ʒe & þe notories* **A** (ɪɪ 91). ᴏᴇᴅ records *nysot* "wanton girl" from Skelton; the word here (perhaps in apposition to *notaryes*) seems to be more generally "fools."

100   St. Mary's rents are perhaps those paid on the Annunciation: cf. ᴍᴇᴅ *Marie* 1a (d). *sowsest*: see Appendix, p. 124.

102   *faytles*: Kane (p. 436) argues for *feyntles* "untiring" (**A** ɪɪ 94) as the *difficilior lectio* (as opposed to "faithless"), but *faytles* may mean "without deeds": cf. **Z** ɪ 110.

104   *mayde murgust on erthe*: *mulere (maiden* LM*) a maiden (moiller* L*) of gode* (etc.) **A** (ɪɪ 96).

105   *A, he*: both mean "she."

107-108   *lewte ... lawe*: reversed in **A** (ɪɪ 99-100). All **B** ᴍss (and the corrector of **A**-text H²) have *lawe* in both lines.

109   *iuggede*: *iugge (wol iugge*, etc.) **A** (ɪɪ 101). In **Z** this refers to the recent scene which provided a formal legal contract for the marriage; in **A** it refers to the future negotiations in London.

For Consience ys of ys consayl ant knoweth yow vchon*e*,
Ant yf he fynd yow in defawte ant wyt the fals hold,
Hyt schal besytte youre sowle ful sowre at the laste."
¶ Hereto assenthet Cyuyle, ac Symonye ne wolde
115 Tyl he haued syluer for hys seles ant signes togydderes.
Thenne fette Fauel forth florynes ynowe,
Ant bad Gyle [gyue] gold alle abowte
To Symonye ant Cyuyle ant sethe alle the oth*ur*,
| Ant namelyche the notaryes that there noen fayle,
120 Ant feffe False Wytnesse wyt florynes ynowe,
"For he may Mede amaystrye ant make at my wylle."
fol. 128r Tho thys gold was ygyue, gret was the thonkyng
To Fals ant to Fauel for here fayre yft*us*,
Ant com*en* to conforte fram care the false
125 Ant seyden, "**Syre,** c*er*tes, sese schal we ner*e*
Tyl Mede be thy weded wyf thorw wyt of vs alle.
We han Mede amaystred thorw oure m*ur*y speche,
That he **hath** graunted to go w*yth* a god wylle
To Londone, to loke yf that lawe wolde
130 Jugge yow ioyntely in ioye togydderes."
Thenne was Falsenesse fayn ant Fauel as blythe
Ant let sompne al **ys** segges in schyres aboute,
Ant bad hem alle be bow, beggares ant oth*ur*,
To wenden w*yth* hym to Westemynstre to wytnesse thys dede.
135 Thenne kared they for kaples to kayre*n* hem thed*ur*,
| Ac Fauel **bad** feche forth foles **ynowe,**
Ant sette Mede on a scheryue yschoed al newe,
Ant Fals on a sysor that softeliche trotted,
Ant Fauel on fayr speche, fetysliche atyred.

Z 111-117 = **A** 103-109; **Z** 118; **Z** 119-139 = **A** 110-130.

113 sowle: *soulis* **A** (ɪɪ 105).
116-117 Written as one line in **Z**.
117 gyue: *om.* **Z** (haplography); cf. below **Z** ɪɪ 167.
118 Unique to **Z**: cf. below **Z** ɪɪ 168 and note.
125 Syre (all **B** ᴍss): *om.* **A** (ɪɪ 116).
131 *Falsenesse* (most **B** ᴍss, **C** with different word order): *Fals* **A** (ɪɪ 122).
133 bad hem (M, cf. E *þaim*; all **B** ᴍss *bad hem* (except M *bade*), **C**): *om.* **A** (ɪɪ 124).
136 bad feche: *fette* **A** (ɪɪ 127).
   ynowe (most **B** ᴍss, **C**): *of þe beste* **A**. Kane (p. 436) argues against *forþ*.
139 fetysliche: Kane (p. 436) argues in favour of *feintliche* "feignedly" (**A** ɪɪ 130).

140 ¶ Thenne haued notaryes none, anuyed they were,
         For Symonye ant Cyuyle scholde goen on here fete.
         Thenne swor Cyuyle ant seyde by the rode
         That sompnoures scholde be sadeled ant serue **Symonye,**
         "Ant lat aparayle the prouisoures in palfrayes wyse:
145   Syre Symonye hymsylf schal sytte on here bak*us*,
         For denes schull*e* ben dyght as destreres –
       | They schal bere thes byschopes **tyl they be there.**
         Erchdeken*us* officiales, Y hote that they ben atyred,
         For they schul serue mysylf that Cyuyle hatte;
150   Ant lat kartsadle the commessarye, oure kart schal he draw
         Ant fetten oure vitayles of fornicatores,
         Ant maketh Lyare a lankart to lede alle thys oth*ur*
         As fobbes ant faytoures that on here fet rennes."
       | Thenne Fals fareht forth ant Fauel togyderes,
155   Ant Mede in the mydd*us* ant alle thys men aft*ur*.
         I haue no tome to telle the tayl that he*m* folewed
         Of many man*ere* men that on thys mold libbes,
         Ac Gyle was forgoar ant **gyde hem to lede.**
       | **Ac** Sothnesse sey hym wel, seyde but lyte,
160   **Ac fiched hym faste ant goth afore alle**

Z 140-147 = **A** 131-138; **Z** 148; **Z** 149-159 = **A** 140-150; **Z** 160 (cf. **A** 151).

141   *For* (all **B** mss except F): *þat* (etc.) **A** (ii 132).

143   *Symonye: hem ichone* **A** (ii 134).

144   This may be part of the narrative (*lat* pret. 3 sg.) or part of Civil's speech (*lat* imperative); Kane takes it as the latter.

146   *denes:* most **A** mss (except JWN) add *& southdenis*, which gives a metrically more satisfactory line.

147   *tyl they be there: & bringe hem at reste* **A** (ii 138), which improves the alliterative pattern.

148   Here **A** (ii 139) has *Paulynes peple for pleyntes in constorie* (= **B** ii 178) (cf. note to **Z** ii 80 above), but **B** (ii 174) has *Erchedekenes and Officials and alle youre Registrers.* Thus **B** has both the **Z** line (in part) and the **A** line.

153   Kane (p. 436) argues for *fobbis* but also for *iotten* against *rennes* (etc.).

154   **A** (ii 145) reads: *Fals & fauel fariþ forþ togidere.*

156   *tome:* supported by Kane (p. 162 ff.).

158   *gyde hem to lede: gyede hem alle* **A** (ii 149).

160   **A** (ii 151) has: *But prikede forþ on his palfray & passide hem alle,* a much stronger line.
         fiched "braced himself in the saddle": see MED *fichen* v.(1) 1(a) refl.

Ant com to the kying*u*s court ant Consyence tolde.
Ant Conscience to the king carped yt aft*u*r,
Ant how thys corsed companie that to the court wolde,
Of Symonye, of Cyuyle, ant seyde hym al togyderes
165 **How Fauel ant Falsenesse fondet to lach Mede**
To maryage, ant on wat man*e*re hym lette,
Ant how Gyle gaf the gold to gomes abowte
To Symonye, to Cyuyle, ant seyde al togyderes,
Ant how Teologye tened hym ant traytowres hem called,
170 **Ant seyde Trewthe for here trespas scholde tene hem vch one.**
 | "By Cryst," qu*a*d kyng tho, "ant Y cache myghte
fol. 128v   Fals oth*u*r Fauel or eny of here feres,
Y wyl be wreke of tho wrech*u*s that wyrche*n* so hylle,
Ant do hange hem by the hals ant alle that he*m* menthyneth.
175 Schal neuer*e* man on this molde mempryse the leste,
But ryght as lawe loketh lat fal on hem alle
For eny m*e*rcy of Mede, by Marye of heuene!"
Ant comawnded a constable that com at the furst
To atache tho tyrauntes, "for eny tresor, Y hote!
180 Fet*u*reth Falsenesse faste for eny skynes yftes,
Ant gurdeth of Gyeles heued – lat hym go no forth*u*r –
Ant bryngeth Mede to me mawgre hem alle.

Z 161-162 = **A** 152-153; **Z** 163-170; **Z** 171-176 = **A** 154-159; **Z** 177; **Z** 178-182 = **A** 160-164.

163-170   These lines, unique to **Z**, summarize the action of Passus II up to this point; they are redundant and were properly omitted in the **A** revision. The syntax is uneven, suggesting an incomplete draft: "(and told him) how this cursed company that wanted to go to court, (and told him) of Simony and Civil, and told him altogether how Favel and Falseness attempted to bring Meed to marriage, and in what manner he was prevented (*or* how to prevent him), and how Guile gave the gold to men all around, to Simony, to Civil, and told him altogether (*but see note to 168*), and how Theology was angry and called them traitors, and said that Truth would be angry with all of them for their trespass."

167-168   Cf. above **Z** II 117-118.

168   *ant seyde al togyderes*: probably the result of dittography from 164; the corresponding line (118) reads *ant sethe alle the othur*.

171   *kyng*: *þe king* **A** (II 154); for the omission of the definite article, cf. below **Z** III 17 and Appendix, p. 125.

173   *wyl* (J): *wolde* (etc.) **A** (II 156).

175   Kane (p. 436) supports *leste* but argues for *of* against *on*.

177   Unique to **Z**.

179   *To*: *To a* **Z**.

¶ Symonye, **sey hym** Y sende hym to warne
  That Holy Chyrche for hym worth harmed for euere;
185| Ant thow lache Lyare, lat hym nat askape
  Tyl he be pot on the pylory for eny preyere, Y hote."
  Drede at the dore stod ant the dyne herde,
  How the kyng konstables comaunded ant oth*ur*,
  As *ser*iauntes ant scheryues that schyres han to kepe;
190 **Warned Fals fore ant ys feres alle.**
  Thenne Falsenesse for fere fley to the freres.
 | Gyle doth hym to, agast for to dye,
 | Ac marchawns mette w*yth* hym, made hym abyde,
  Byschutten hym in here schoppe to schewen here war*e*;
195 P*a*rayled hym as a prentys, the peple to *ser*ue.
  Lyghtlyche Lyare lep away thenne,
  Lurkynge thorw lanes, toluged of mony.
  He was nawer welcome for ys mony tales,
  But ouer al yhonted ant yhote trusse,
200| Tyl pardoners haued pyte, polled hym into howse,
 | Wosche*n* ant wyped hym, wownden hym in clout*us*,
 | Ant sente*n* hym Sone*n*day*us* w*yth* seles to chirches,
  Ant gaf pardoun*e* for pans poundmele aboute.
  Thenne lowred leches ant letres they hym sent
205 For to wonye w*yth* hem, wateres to loke.
  Spisores speke to hym to spyen h*er*e **thyng*us*,**

Z 183-187 = **A** 165-169; **Z** 188-189; **Z** 190 = **A** 170 + 171; **Z** 191-206 = **A** 172-187.

---

  183 *Symonye sey hym* (cf. N *Sey symonye & cyuyle*): *Symonye & cyuyle* **A** (ıı 165). "As for Simony, tell him that I am sending to advise him...." The capitulum mark has been badly placed, as though it meant "Simony saw...."

  187 *dyne*: found in a few **A** mss, against the majority *doom*. **C** has *duene* "din," **B** *doom*. Kane (p. 437) hesitantly adopts *doom*, suggesting **C**-text contamination of JVL or independent variation. On our hypothesis, *dyne* is original (preserved in JVL and **C**) and *doom* is the revision.

  188-189 These lines refer back to 178, adding sheriffs and sergeants; they are omitted in **A** (cf. the omission of **Z** ıı 163-170), but partly preserved in **B** ıı 209.

  190 Expanded into two lines in **A** (ıı 170-171).

  192 Unless *doth hym to* can mean "pulls himself together," insert *go* after *to* as in **A** (ıı 173).

  194 *schoppe* (D, some **B** mss): *shoppis* **A** (ıı 175).

  206 *thyngus*: *ware* **A** (ıı 187); the **A** reading is more specific.

For he kowthe of here craft ant knew mony gum̄mes;
Ac mynstrales ant messageres mette w*yth* hym ones
Ant helden hym half yere ant eleue dayes.
210   Freres w*yth* fayre speche fette*n* hym thennes;
For knowyng of comares coped hym as a frere,
Ac he hath leue to lepe out as ofte as hym licut
| Ant ys welcome wen a wol, woneth w*yth* hem ofte.
Alle fledde for fere, **saue Fauel ant Mede,**
215   **Ac bothe to trembled, atached tho they were.**

Z 207-214 = **A** 188-195; **Z** 215.

214-215   Expanded into four lines in **A** (ii 195-198). The capture of Favel conflicts
with iii 1, and is omitted in **A**. *to* may be "two" or "then" (= *tho*) or the prefix
    to- of an unrecorded **to-tremble.*
    tho "when."

Passus Tercius

Now ys Mede the mayde, ant no mo of hem alle,
Wyth bedles ant bayles ybrought to the king.
The kyng cald a clerk, Y can nat ys name,
To take Mede the mayde ant maken here at ese.

fol. 129r "Y schal assay here mysylf ant sothelyche apose
6   Wat man of thys world that here were leuest;
Ant yf he wyrche by wyt ant my wille folwe,
Y wille fo[r]gyue here **that** gult, so me God helpe."
| Corteyseliche **thys** clerk, as the kyng hyghte,
10   **Ladde this lady to lofte, that Mede his yhote.**
Ac there was murthe ant mynstracie Mede to plese:
That wonyeth at Westmenstre wurcheped here alle.
Gentelyche wyth ioye the justises **monye**
Busked hem to the bour there the buyrde dweld;
15   Conforted here kyndelyche by cleregyus leue,
Seyden, "Mourne nat, Mede, ne mak thow no sorwe,
| For we wyl wysse kyng ant thy way schape
For to wedde at thy wille were thow lef licuth,
For al conscienses cast ant craft, as we trowe."
20   Myldelyche Mede mercyed hem alle
Of theyr grete godnesse, ant gaf hem vchone
Coupus of clene gold, coppus of syluer,

Z III 1-17 = A III 1-9 (10) 11-17; Z 18; Z 19-22 = A 18-21.

---

6   *world*: supported by Kane (p. 437) on A II 6.

8   *forgyue: fo gyue* Z.

10   A (III 10) has: *Tok mede be þe myddel & brouȝte hire to chaumbre.*

13   *monye* (one B MS): *somme / sone* (etc.) A (III 13); Kane (p. 437) adopts *somme* as the *difficilior lectio*.

17   *kyng: þe king* A (III 17); see above Z II 171 and note.

18   = B III 18 (C IV 19, with *wende* for *wedde*): om. A.

22   *coppus* (W, most B MSS, C): *pecis* A (III 21) and two B MSS. Kane (p. 158) argues in favour of *coppus* "copes" but does not adopt it.

Rynges w*yth* rubyes ant rychesses monye,
The leste mon of here meyne a mote*n* of gold.
25 Thenne law3te they leue, this lord*us*, at Mede.
W*yth* that come clerk*us*, **conforted** here the same
Ant beden here be blythe, "for we beth thyn owne
For to wyrche thy wylle, wyle **thow my3t loke**."
Hendelyche he thenne byhyghte hem the same,
30 "To loue yow lelely **wyle my lyf deureth,**
Ant in the consistorye at court do calle youre name
Ant bugge benefices were yow best lycuth,
Porchase prouendres thereto, wyle my pans lasteth.
| Schal no lowedenesse lette hem that Y louye
35 That they **nar** furst avau*n*sed, for Yc am yknowe
| There conny*n*gge clerk*us* **cleketh** byhyend."
¶ The kyyng fro consayl com, kalde aft*ur* Mede
Ant ofsent [hire] as swythe. *S*eriauns here fette

Z 23-31 = **A** 22-30; **Z** 32-33; **Z** 34-36 = **A** 31-33; [om. **A** 34-89]; **Z** 37-38 = **A** 90-91.

---

26 *conforted* (three **B** MSS): *to conforten* (etc.) **A** (III 25).

28 *thow my3t loke* (cf. *þow my3t laste* in several **B** MSS): *þi (oure) lif lastiþ (duriþ*, etc.) **A** (III 27); see Kane, p. 437. For *loke* "have the use of one's faculties, be alive," see the phrase *liven and/or loken* in MED *loken* 2(a).

30-31 In direct speech also in some **A** and **B** MSS.

30 *wyle my lyf deureth:* & *lordis hem (3ou) make* **A** (III 29); cf. **A** III 27.

32-33 = **C** IV 33, 32. In two **A** MSS (WN) they are placed after **A** III 33 (**Z** III 36), where they are syntactically awkward. Kane (p. 33) argues that in WN they are inept insertions from **C**, where they follow what is **Z** III 30. They may, however, have survived in WN from the **Z** version but have been misplaced; if they were misplaced in the **A** archetype, this would account for their removal from the other manuscripts. See Introduction, p. 25.

32 *were yow best lycuth: pluralite to haue* **C** (IV 33).

34 *lette hem: hym lette þe lede* **A** (III 31).

35 *nar: ne worþ* **A** (III 32). *Yc* written *y^c*.

36 *cleketh: shuln clokke* (etc.) **A** (III 33). The word *clokke* is usually taken (after Skeat) from OF *cloquer* "limp," and in view of the frequent *e/o* confusion (Introduction, p. 31) this interpretation would be possible. On the other hand, if *conny*n*gge* is taken in a pejorative sense, cf. OED *clack* v¹ "cluck" of birds chattering: the image of "crafty" clerks clucking like hens after Meed is a pleasing one. After 36 **A** (and subsequent versions) has Meed's confession to the friar, her window-glazing offer, the poet's attack on avarice (especially in the victualling trade), and the interchange between Meed and the Mayor (**A** III 34-89).

38 *ofsent hire: of sentare* **Z**. See Introduction, p. 31, for aural errors.

Ant browghte here to boure w*yth* **a blithe chere.**
40   Corteyslyche the kyng commesed to telle
     To Mede the mayde, meled **his** word*us*:
     "Vnwyttyly thow, womma*n*, wrowt hast ofte,
    | Ac worse wrowghtest nere **as** wen þow Fals toke.
     Ac Y fortgyue that gult ant graunte the grace
45   **Ant fro** hennes to thy deth day do þow so no more.
     I haue a kny3t, Conscience, com lat fro byyonde;
     Yf he wylneth the to wyue, wolte þow hym haue?"
    | "Ye, lord," q*ua*d that lady, "lord hit **me** forbede
     But Y be holy at youre heste – lat hange me ell*us*!"
50 ¶ Thenne was Conscience ycald to come ant apere
     Byfor the kyng ant ys consayl of clerk*us* ant oth*ur*.
     Kneled Conscience ant to the kyng lowted,
     Ant wat that ys wille were ant wat he do scholde.
     "Wylt þow wedde thys **lady, ant** Y wyl assente?
fol. 129v   For he ys fayn of thy fellawschippe ant for to be thy make."
56   Quad Consciense to the kyng, "Cryst hit me forbede!
     Ar Y wedded such a wyf, wo me bytyde!
     Sche ys frele of here fayth, fikel of here speche.
     A maketh men mysdo many score tyme.
60   In triste of here tresor he teneht ful monye;
     Wyues ant wedew*us* wantownesse he thechet,
     Lereth hem lecherye that loueyeth here yft*us*.
     Youre fader a feld thorw false byheste;
     Poyseneth popes, apeyreth holy chirche.
65   Ys nat a bettre bawde, by hym that me made,
     Bytwene heuene ant helle ant erthe thow me sowte.
     Sche ys tykel of here tayl, talewys of tonge,

Z 39-67 = **A** 92-120.

39   *a blithe chere*: *blisse & wiþ ioye* (etc.) **A**.
42   *womman*: Kane (p. 164) argues for *wy* as the *difficilior lectio*.
43   *þow* spelled *yow* (as in 45, 47, 54); see Introduction, p. 31.
46   Some A mss have *hatte* after *kny3t*: Kane (p. 438) argues against it.
48   *forbede: forbede ellis* **A** (iii 101).
52   *kneled (knelyd þo* J): *knelynge* **A** (omitting *ant*) (iii 105).
54   *lady: womman* **A** (iii 107).
  ant: 3if **A**.
57   *wedded* (J): *wedde* **A** (iii 110).

As comewn as the cartway to knaues ant to alle,
To monek*us*, to mynst*r*ales, to myseles in hegges,
70   Sysoures ant sompneres, such men here preyseth.
A doth men lesen here land, **ye** ant here lyf bothe.
Scheryues of schires were schent yf he nere,
| **For** he lat passe prysones, payeth for hem ofte:
A gyueth the gaylares gold ant grot*us* togyderes,
75   To vnfetere the fals, fle were hym licut;
| Taketh Trewthe by the top, **tethereth** hym faste,
Ant hangeth hym for hatrede that harmed nere.
To be corsed in the consistorye a cownteth nat a rysch*e*,
| **For** a copeth the comyssarye, coteth ys clerc*us*;
80   Sche ys assoyled thus sone as heresilf licuth.
He may ney as myche do in a monthe on*us*
As youre secrete sel in syxe scor dayes;
For he ys pryue w*yth* the pope, p*r*ouisores hit knoweth,
For Symonye ant heresilf aseleth here bull*us*.
85   A blesseth thes byschop*us*, thow they be lewed;
Prouendreth p*a*rsones, prestes he meynteneth,
To **habbe** le*m*manes ant luttebys all*e* here lyf days
Ant bryngeth forth barnes ayeyn forbode lawes.
There he ys wel w*yth* **a** kyng, wo his the rewme,
90   For he ys fauorable to Fals ant falleth **ryght** ofte.
Barones ant burgeys he bryngeth into sorwe.
By *Jesus*, w*yth* here jueles youre iustyses a schendeth
| Ant lythth ayeyn lawe ant lette hem the gate,
That fayth may nat haue ys forth, here floreynes goth so thykke;
95   The mase for a mene man, thou3 a mote euere,
W*ythoute*n mony or mede or morgage ys land*us*:

Z 68-70 = A 121-123; Z71 = A 125; Z 72 = A 124; Z 73-94 = A 126-147; Z 95 = A 149;
Z 96.

71-72   Reversed in A (III 125, 124). The Z order (with *For* in 73) works well: the
sheriffs benefit financially from Meed's release of prisoners.
76   *tethereth*: *tei3eþ* (*fettreth*) A (III 129).
87   *habbe* (*haue* all B MSS): *holde* A (III 140).
90   *falleth ryght ofte*: *fouliþ* (*falliþ* H) *treuþe ofte* A (III 143). In Z *he* probably refers to
the king, but if *he* = "she," as in A, *falleth* must mean "cause to fall' (MED *fellen*).
95-100   The order in A is: 99, 95, 97, 98, 100 (III 149-151, 148, 152).
96   Unique to Z: "without money or meed or (unless he) mortgage his lands."

Lawe ys so lordlyche ant loth to make hynde.

W*ytho*ute*n* *presentus* or pans a pleseth ful fewe;

He lat lawe as here lust, ant louedays makuth;

100   Clergyse ant coueytyse he coupleth togydere.

Thys ys the lyf of that lady. Now lord yf here sorwe,

Ant alle that meyntyneth here men meschaunce hem bytyde!

For pore men han no pouer to pleyne hem, they hey smerte:

Such a mays*ter* ys Mede among men of gode."

fol. 130r | Thenne morned Mede, mened here to the kyng

106   To haue space to speke, spede yf a myghte.

The kynge graunted here g*ra*ce w*yth* a god wylle:

"Excuse yf thow canst, Y can no more **schewen,**

| For Conscience akusseth to congey the for euer*e*."

110   "Nay, lord," q*ua*d that lady, "leue hym̀ the worse,

Wen [ye] wyte*n* wyt*ur*ly were the wrong lyges.

There that meschef ys gret, Mede may helpe;

Ant thow knowest, Conscience, Y com nat to chyde

Ne to depraue thy p*er*sone w*yth* a proud herte.

115   Wel thow wost, **weye,** but yf tow wyl **gabbe.**

Thow hast hanged on myn half elleuene tymes,

Ant eke ygrype my gold, gef hit were thow lyked.

Ac wy thow wratheste the now, wndor me thynkeuth,

For yut Y may as Y myghte me*n*ske the w*yth* yft*us*,

120   Ant **multiplye** thy monhede more thenne thow knowest.

Ac thow hast defamed me foule afor the kyng here;

That thow seydest, for soth schalt thow nere fynde:

For me were leuere by oure lord to lygge*n* in peyne

Z 97-98 = **A** 150-151; **Z** 99 = **A** 148; **Z** 100-121 = **A** 152-173; **Z** 122-123.

97   *hynde* "end": MED records the spelling *inde*.

103   *they* "though"; *hey* is not **Z**'s usual form for the 3rd person plural pronoun: it may be an error for *they* or *hem*.

108   *schewen*: *seiʒe* (etc.) **A** (III 160).

111   *ye*: *the* **Z**, through incorrect interpretation of *y* as *þ*: see Introduction, p. 31.

115   *weye*: *consience* (etc.) **A** (III 167).
   gabbe (**BC**): *leiʒe* **A** (corr. to *gabbe* H²).

116   *half*: some **A** and **B** MSS have *hals* (two **A** MSS have *nekke*), as does **C**; the variation is textually insignificant and arises solely from confusion between *s/f*.

118   The suffix in *thynkeuth* appears to combine -*eth* and -*uth*.

120   *multiplye*: *maynteyne* **A** (III 172).

122-124   Unique to **Z**.

Wyle that thys world last, the*n* wyrche*n* so ylle.
125 For kyld Y nere no king, ne consayled thereaft*ur*,
    Ne dede as thow demyst – Y do yt on the kynge.
    In Normawndye nas a nat anuyed for my sake;
| Ac thow thysylf sothelyche schamedest ofte,
    Crope into kaban for cold of thy nayles,
130 Wendest that wynt*ur* wolde last euere;
| Draddyst **the to dey** for a dymme clowde
    Ant hastedest hammard for hung*ur* of thy wombe.
    W*yth*oute pyte, thow pylor, pore men thow robbedest,
    Ant bere here bras at thy bak to Kaleys to sylle.
135 There Y lefte w*yth* my lord, ys lyf for to saue,
    Ant made ys **men murye ant** mournyng to leue.
    Y battered hem on the bak, boldede here herte,
    Dede hem hoppe for hope to haue me at wylle.
    Haued Y be marchal of ys men, by Mary of heuene,
140 Y durst haue leyd my lyf ant no lasse wedde,
    A scholde haue be lord of that lond a lengthe ant of brede,
    Ant eke kyng of that kyth, ys kyn for to helpe –
    Ye, the leste brol of ys blod a barones pere.
    Kowardelyche thow, Conscience, conseylest hym thennes,
145 To leuen ys lordschepe for a litel syluer
    That ys the rychest rewme that reyn ouer houes.
    Ac, Conscience, Cryst wot, as Y can descryue,

Z 124; Z 125-146 = A 174-195; [om. A 196-276]; Z 147.

128 *schamedest* "were ashamed"; in A *hym* is added (III 177) so that it means "brought shame on the king."

131 *the to dey*: *to be ded* A (III 180).

133 *thow pylor*: *thow pyte thow pylor* Z. The scribe has placed the words *thow robbedest* at the beginning of 134, perhaps thinking that 133 (in its unemended form) was long enough for a verse line. For other examples of the untrustworthiness of Z's line division, see Introduction, p. 31.

136 *ys men murye* (all B MSS (*meene* H); cf. EM (*alle*) *his merie men*): *hym merþe* A (III 185).

141 *kyng* cancelled before *lord* in Z.

144 *conseylest* (one B MS): *conceiledest* (etc.) A (III 193). The present tense is probably an error, but could have some historical significance.

147-176 In place of these lines, in which Meed continues her denunciation of Conscience (often beyond the reasonable limits of the allegory) to the end of the Passus, the A text (III 196-276) has the rebuttal by Conscience, who defines the two kinds of Meed.

          Out of Northfolk or Normawndye thy name was yfounde.

          For thow canst selle the cow y calf ant wythouten,

150   Halden wyth hym ant wyth here, ay as the licuth.

          Freres fyndeth the a frend that thow furst blamedest:

          Thyselue art asentaunt that they schal men schryue.

          Furst thow corue hem a cope, Conscience, thyselue,

          Ant comawndest vche couent coueytyse to lete,

fol. 130v   Ant nyme nat of no man but as nede hascheth.

156   Now ast thow coped hem in coueytyse, ant cumseth to ryde.

          That weren woned to wade in wynteres ful colde,

          Now beth they boted, tho bewsoun, ant bayard stowlyche bestrydeth.

          The bourlyokest bornet ant blanket to selle,

160   They byggen hyt, nat beggen hit, to bakken thereinne.

          In delys of lecherye ys lycam achoceth

          That such wedus wereth, Y wyl yt avowe.

          For lecherye ys delyt, ant eke aloft bothe

          Letred ant vnlered lewdelyche thow techest:

165   Vnnethe ys ther eny man that nolde be ryche,

Z 148-165.

148   On the satirical allusions to Norfolk (cf. **Z** v 98), eliminated in the **A** text, see Introduction, pp. 16-17.

149   "You can sell the cow whether in calf or not," apparently a proverbial phrase for double-dealing.

151 ff.   Conscience has not "blamed" the friars in this poem. The point of 151-152 is that at one time the friars were rebuked by some authority, represented by Conscience, but have now been allowed to resume their old privileges, such as hearing confession. This could refer to almost any stage in the disputes between the friars and the secular clergy (supported often by the monks and the University of Oxford). In 153 ff. Meed means that the mendicant orders were originally genuinely poor but have become worldly, greedy, and easy-living.

156   *cumseth*: i.e., the friars. Cf. **A** Pr 58, **B** xx 58.

157-158   "Those that used to walk, full cold, in winter, are now booted, those fine fellows, and firmly bestride a fine horse (Bayard)." *bewsoun* is a *hapax legomenon*: cf. *bealle sone*, cited in MED *bel* adj. (a).

159-160   "They don't beg but buy the thickest burnet or blanket that there is for sale, to clothe their backs in." See MED *bornet, blanket*. The only other example of *bakken* in this sense is in **A**-text xi 188.

161-162   "He that wears such clothes, I can safely assert, chokes his body in the delights of lechery."

163-164   "For lechery is delight, and also you teach both lettered and unlettered men lewdly (incorrectly);" the sense of *aloft* is not clear and possibly conceals a corruption.

Ant alle the wytt*us* that a wot to wynnygge he schapeth.
Of alle man*e*re men Mede ys desyred;
Conscience but at consayl countheth ful fewe:
Marchauns myghte forbere the, none man bettre.

170   Conscience in couetyse clerc*us* hath robed,
Ant soyleth men for syluer, we sen wel ouresylue.
Conscience ys the cumsyng of alle skynes werk*us*:
Be hyt wel, be hit wo, a wot hyt at the furst.
Ys maystry ys aboue me that Mede am yhote.

175   W*yth*outen hys wyt wyrch Y not, God wot the sothe,
That thow ne art furst found*ur*: god fayth it knoweth."

Z 166-176.

166 *a* "he." For *wynnygge*, see Appendix, p. 123.

167 For the sentiment, cf. **A** III 196-214.

168 "Conscience reckons few (supporters) except at council," presumably ironic.

170 Cf. **Z** III 156.

172-176 "Conscience is the beginning of every kind of deed; whether it is good or ill, he knows it at the start; his authority is greater than mine, Meed's. Without his knowledge I do not do anything − God knows the truth − of which you are not the first founder. Good faith knows it." Meed argues that Conscience is at the root of all human decisions, of which Meed is only one manifestation.

Passus Quartus

"Seseth, **seseth**," sayde the kynge, "Y soffre yow no leng*ur*:
Ye schal sawtene for sothe ant s*er*ue me bothe.
Kysse h*ere*," q*ua*d the kyng, "Conscience, Y hote!"
"Nay, by Cryst," q*ua*d Conscience, "congeye me **arre**!
5   But Resoun radde me thertyl, rather wyll Y deye."
"Ant Y comawnde," q*ua*d the kyng to Consciencie thenne,
"Rape the to ryde ant Resoun that thow feche.
Comawnde hym that he come my consayl to here,
| For he schal rewle my rewme, rede me the beste
10 Of Mede ant mo oth*ur* ant wat man schal here wedde,
Ant kounte w*yth* the, Conscyence, so me Cryst helpe,
How thow lerest the peple, lered ant lewed."
"Y am fayn of þ*at* forward," seyth the freke thenne,
And ryt ryght to Resoun ant rowneth in ys here;
15 Seyde hym as the kying sente ant senes tok ys leue.
"I schal araye me to ryde," q*ua*d Resoun, "reste the the wil."
Ant cald Tomme Trewe-tonge-telle-me-no-tal*us*-
Ne-lesyng*us*-to-law3e-of-for-Y-loued-hit-nere.
"Sette my sadel vp on Suffre-tyl-Y-se-my-tyme,
20 Ant lat warryoke **Wyl** wyth **stronge wytty** gurth*us*.
Honge on hym the heuye brydel to holde ys heued lowe,

Z ɪv 1-16 = **A** ɪv 1-16; [om. **A** 17]; **Z** 17-18; **Z** 19-21 = **A** 18-20.

---

4   *arre: rapere* **A** (ɪv 4).

12 *lered ant lewed: þe lerid & þe lewid* **A** (ɪv 12).

14 *ryt*: Kane (p. 439) argues that *renneþ* is the *difficilior lectio*.

16 After this line **A** has ɪv 17:
        And calde catoun his knaue, curteis of speche

17-18   These lines (= **B** ɪv 18-19, **C** v 18-19) are also in mss EAWM of the A-text, which also have **A** ɪv 17 (as do the **B** and **C** texts).

20   *Wyl*: if this is the personification of *Voluntas*, the allegory fits well with lines 21-22. **A** (ɪv 19) has *hym wel*: the **Z** scribe could have omitted *hym*; for *wyl* = "well," cf. **Z** ɪv 89.

    stronge wytty gurthus (*witty wordes gerþes* most **B** mss): *wytful* (or *ri3tful*) **A** (ɪv 19).

For yut wyl he make mony a wehe ar we be there."
Thenne Conscyence on ys kapel kayres forth faste,
Ant Resoun ryt **forth** w*yth* hym **ryght to the kyng.**

25 Ac on Wareyn Wysdom ant Wytty ys fere

fol. 131r Folwed hem faste, for they haued to done
In the cheker ant in chaunserye, to be descharged of thyng*us*;
Ant ryde*n* faste, for Resoun schold rede hem the beste
For to saue*n* hemsylf fro schame ant fro harmes.

30 Ac Conscyence com arst to court by a myle
Ant romed forth w*yth* Resoun ryght to the kyng.
Corteyslyche the [kyng tho] com aye Resoun,
Ant bytwene hymsylf ant ys sone sette hym a benche,
Ant worden ful wysly a gret wyle togyderes.

35 Thenne com Pes in the p*ar*lement ant potte vp a bille,
How Wronge ayeyne ys wylle haued ys wyf take,
Ant how a rauessched Rose, Reynald*us* loue,
Ant Margrete of here maydenhod maugre here chec*us*:
"Bothe my ges ant my grys ys gadelynges fecheth;

40 Y dar nat for fere of hym fyghte ne chyde.
| A borwed of me bayard ant broughte ayeyn nere,
Ne no ferthyng therefore, for hought Y cowthe plede.
A meynteyneth ys men to morthr*e* myn hewes;
Forstalleth my fayres, fyghteth in my chepyng,

45 Brekth vp my bern*us* dore, berth awey my wete,
| Taketh me but a tayle for ten quart*er* otes,
| Ant yut a bat me thereto, lyth be my mayde.
Y nam nat hardy for hym vnnethe to loke."
The kyng knewe he seyde sothe, for Conscyence hym tolde,

50 **Ant Sothenesse swor hit was sothe that he tolde.**
Ant thenne was Wronge wo ant Wysdom a sought

Z 22-49 = **A** 21-48; **Z** 50; **Z** 51 = **A** 49.

24 *ryght to the kyng: and rapiþ hym swype* **A** (ɪv 23); the **A** reading is more vigorous.
32 *kyng tho* (JM): om. **Z**, probably by haplography.
41 *ayeyn nere (hym ageyn neuere* one **B** ᴍs): *him neuere aȝen* (etc.) **A** (ɪv 40).
45 *bernus* (so some **B** ᴍss): attributive singular in **A** (ɪv 44).
47 *bat* (V): *betiþ* **A** (ɪv 46).
48 *vnnethe to loke*: supported by Kane (p. 439).
50 Unique to **Z**. For the character Soothness, see Introduction, p. 16.
51 *Ant thenne was Wronge wo: Wrong was aferd þo* **A** (ɪv 49).

        To make ys pays w*yth* ys pans ant p*ro*fred hym monye,

| Ant seyde, "Haued Y loue of my lord, lytel wold Y rech

        Thow Pes ant ys pouer pleynen hem euere."

55   Wysdom wan tho ant so dede Wyt alse,

        For that Wrong haued ywrought so wyked a dede,

        Ant warned Wrong tho w*yth* such a wys tale:

        "Ho so wyrcheth be wyl, wrathe maketh ofte.

        Y seg by thysylf, thow schalt hyt sone fynde:

60   But yf Mede hit make, thy meschef ys vppe;

        Bothe thy lyf ant thy lond*us* lyth in ys grace."

        Wrong thenne on Wysdom weped faste

        To helpe hym for his [   ] ant handi-dandy payed.

        Thenne Wysdom and Wyt went*en* togyderes

65   An nom*en* Mede **myd** hem m*er*cy to wynne.

        Pes potte forth ys heued an his panne blody:

        "W*yth*out*en* gult, God wot, gat Y this scathe."

        Conscience ant the kyng knewe wel the sothe

        Ant wysten wel that Wrong was a schrewe euer*e*.

70   Ac Wysdom ant Wyt were aboute faste

        To ouercome the kyng **thorw** catel yf they myghte.

        The kyng swor by Cryst ant by ys crowne bothe

        That Wrong for ys werc*us* schold wo tholye,

        Ant comawnded a constable to caste hym in yrenes:

Z 52-74 = **A** 50-72.

    52   *monye* "money" (?): this is the reading of five **A** MSS, but Kane (and the **B**-text) read *manye* (i.e., "many pennies").

    53   *my lord* (one **B** MS, *the lorde* **C**): *my lord þe king* **A** (IV 51).

    54   *pleynen*: *pleynide* **A** (IV 52).

    59   *thysylf*: Kane (p. 439) argues for *myself*.

    61   *londus*: *lond* **A** (IV 59).

    62   *faste* (W): *hym to helpe* (etc.) **A** (IV 60).

    62-63   This is a noted crux in the A-text. Some MSS divide the lines as **Z** does, others divide after *helpe* (*hym*). In line 63 editors, relying on MSS TH²Ch, read *For of hise penys he proffride handy dandy to paye*; Skeat reads *Him for his handidandi rediliche he payede*. As Kane remarks, "the problem is to account for the loss of *penys he proffride* from so many manuscripts." If **Z** represents the earliest version, then the line must be retained as it is in **Z** and in most **A** MSS. Either Langland never completed it, or the unknown rules of "handy-dandy" may have included a phrase such as "help him for his, help me for mine."

    65   *myd* (most **B** MSS, **C**): *wiþ* **A** (IV 63). Kane (p. 158) notes that *myd* would improve the metre but "lacks authority" (i.e., among **A** MSS).

    71   *thorw* (**C**): *wiþ* **A** (IV 69).

75   "A schal nat this vij yer yse ys fete ones."

fol. 131v   "God wot," quad Wysdom, "that were nat the beste.

Ant he amendes mowe make, lat meynprise hym haue

| Ant be borw for ys bale, beggen hym **mercy;**

Amende that a mysdede, ant eueremore the bettre."

80   Wyt acordede therewyth ant seyde the same:

"Beture ys that bote bale adown brynge

Then bale be ybete ant bote nere the bettre."

Thenne gan Mede to meke here ant mercy **a** bysowte,

Ant profred Pes a present alle of puyre gold

85   **Ant seyde,** "Haue thys of me to amendy thy scath,

For Y wyl wage for Wrong a wyl do so no more."

| Pyteuselyche Pees thenne preyed the kynge

To haue mercy on that [man that] mysdede hym ofte:

"For he hath wageth me wyl, as Wysdom hym taughte;

90   Y forgyue hym that gult wyth a god wylle.

So that ye assente, Y can sey no more,

For Me[de] hath made my mendus, Y may no more aske."

¶ "Nay," quad the kynge tho, "so God yf me blysse,

Wrong wendet nat so away ar Y wyte more.

95   Lope he so lyghtly awey, lawen a wolde

Ant hef the balder to be to bete myn hewes.

But Resoun haue rewthe on hym, he schal reste hym in my stokus

As longe as Y leue, but the more loue hit make."

Summe raden Resoun to haue rewthe on the screwe

100   Ant to consayle the kyng **for Conscienses sake**

Z 75-100 = **A** 73-98.

78   *mercy*: *bote* **A** (IV 76).

79   *that a mysdede* "what he mis-did," supported by some **A** MSS, but in most **A** MSS *mysdede* is a noun.

83   *a* "she."

85   *Ant seyde* (**Z** only): **A** (IV 83) has *man quaþ heo* after *me*.

87   The word-order is that of most **B** MSS and **C**: **A** differs.

88   *man that*: om. **Z**, by haplography; the syntax is barely tolerable without these words.

89   *wageth* past participle: see Appendix, pp. 117, 122.

92   *Mede*: *me* **Z**.

93   *God*: supported by Kane, who argues (p. 158) against emending for metre.

96   *hef*: presumably = *eft*. **A** MSS divide between *eft/ofte*, discussed by Kane (p. 440).

100   *for Conscienses sake*: *& consience boþe* **A** (IV 98).

That Mede moste be meynper̄nor, Resoun they besow3te.
"Rede me nat," q*u*ad Resoun, "no rew3the to haue
Tyl lord*u*s ant ladyes louyen **in** trewthe,
Ant Pernele pur̄fil be potte in here wyche;

105   Tyl child*u*rne chersyng ben chasted w*yth* yerd*u*s,
Ant harlotes holynesse yholde for an hyne;
Tyl clerk*u*s ant knyt*u*s be corteys of here mowth*e*
Ant h[et]yn harlotrye, to here yt or to mowth hit;
Tyl p*r*estes here p*r*echyng p*r*oue hit **on** hemsylf

110   Ant do hit in dede to drawen vs to gode;
Tyl seynt James be sought there Y schal asyngne,
That no man go to Galys but yf [he] go for euere,
Ant alle Rome rennares for robberes of byyende
To bere no syluer ouer se that sygne of kynge scheweth,

115   Nayther grot*u*s ne gold ygraue w*yth* kyng*u*s croune,
Vp forfeture of that fe, ho so fynt hym at Douere,
But yf [yt] be machaunt or ys man or messager w*yth* letres
Or p*r*este or p*r*ouysor that the pope auaunseth.
Thenne schal Y knele to the kyng ant cryen hym of grace

120   **For Wrong*u*s werc*u*s ant wrathe in hope that he amende:**
In no manere ell*u*s, nat for `no´ manes bysechyng."
Waren Wysdom ant Wytty ys fere

Z 101-118 = **A** 99-116; **Z** 119-121. **Z** 122 (cf. **Z** v 1) = **A** 141.

103   *in*: *alle* **A** (ɪv 101).

104   *Pernele*: two **B** ᴍss have a form without suffixal *-(e)s*. Cf. Appendix, p. 116.

106   *hyne*: Kane (pp. 161-162) argues that *heþyng* (found only in ᴍs Ch) is the *difficilior lectio* but its senses (ᴍᴇᴅ 2(d)) do not seem to fit the meaning required here, nor is *hyne* in this sense (ᴍᴇᴅ 2(c)) common enough to be an easy scribal substitution.

108   *hetyn*: *hteyn* **Z**.

112   *he*: om. **Z**.

115   *croune*: Kane (p. 440) argues that *coyn* in the sense "stamp, impress" is the *difficilior lectio*, but scribes could as easily have substituted *coyn* in its ordinary sense.

117   *yt*: om. **Z**.

118   *preste or prouysor* (*prestis oþer prouisours* H): *prouisour or prest* (etc.) **A** (ɪv 116).
      auuanseth cancelled after *pope* **Z**.

119-121   Unique to **Z**.

122 ff.   On the **Z** narrative from here to the end of the Passus, see Introduction, p. 14. It is, in its own right, a perfectly coherent story, if the text is corrected at line 132. Its problems include: the repetition of **Z** 122 ff. at the beginning of Passus v (the relative position the lines occupy in the A-text) and the inconsistency at **Z** 158-159: both these features show the Z-version in the process of revision towards the A-text.

Cowthe nat warpe a word tho to wy*th*segge Resoun,
But stoden stylle as stuty hors that dolleth.
125 **Conscience ant the kyng acorded to Resoun**
fol. 132r   Ant seyden that Resoun ryghtfullyche haued schewed;
"Ac ys hit ful hard, by myn heued, herto to brynge hit,
Alle my lege led*us* to lede hem th*us* euene."
"By hym that raw3te on the rode," q*ua*d Resoun to the kyng,
130 **But yf thow rewle th*us* [thy] rewme, Resoun schal nere."**
"Thow schalt rewle my rewme, Resoun, ant ryde by my syde."
"Nay, redyly," q*ua*d Resoun, "þ[ou] schalt no ryght schewe
Wyle Mede hat the maystrye to mote in thys halle.
Ac Y **schal** schewe ensamples as Y se oth*ur*:
135 **Ac Y sey for mysylf, ant hit so byfelle**
That Y were kinge wy*th* crowne to kepen a rewme,
Scholde nere Wrong in thys world, that Y wyte my3te,
Be vnpensched in my pouer for p*er*yl of my sowle,
Ne gete my grace thorw gyft, so me God helpe;
140 Ne for no mede haue m*er*cy, but mekenesse hit maked.

Z 123-130 (cf. **Z** v 2-9) = **A** 142 (143-144) 145-148 (149); **Z** 131; **Z** 132-140 = **A** (117) 118-125.

124-125   Similar to **A** iv 143-144:
          But stariden for stodyenge and stoden as bestis
          Þe king acordite, be crist, to resonis sawis (etc.; cf. **Z** v 3-4).

124   "as a faltering horse that is sluggish." *stuty* (a nonce-word), apparently related to *stotay(e)* v. "falter, totter, come to a stand," *stutte* (a West-Midland word) "stop, cease," and *stut* v.[1] 2 "stumble" (OED 1573). *dolleth*: see OED *dull* v. II 6 b "be inactive or sluggish."

129 ff.   The king has said (127-128) that it will be hard to rule the kingdom according to Reason's advice. Reason replies (129-130) that unless he does rule it in this way, Reason will never rule it. The king insists that Reason rule by his side (131), to which Reason replies that the king can never dispense justice as long as Meed has mastery and permits Wrong to go unpunished (132-133). In the A-text Reason's long speech is given earlier: the intrusive *quaþ resoun* in **A** iv 117 may be a vestigial trace of the Z version, in which Reason's speech begins at that point.

130   *thy*: om. **Z** (cf. **Z** v 9).

132   *þou*: *y* **Z**. Clearly, for grammatical reasons, either *y* or *schalt* (pres. 2 sg.) must be emended. In the A-text (**A** iv 117) Reason is insisting that he will show no mercy on Wrong: *I shal no reuþe haue*. In **Z**, however, Reason is saying that the king cannot rule justly while Meed is at court.

134   *schal* (one **B** MS): *may* **A** (iv 119).

135   *for*: Kane (p. 440) argues for *be*.
       byfelle: *were* **A** (iv 120).

For [n]ullum malum the man mette **erit** inpunitum
Ant nullum bonum the bolde be irremuneratum.
Lat thy confessor, syre kyng, **kenne** the thys [on] Englis,
Ant yf ye wyrcheth in **dede,** Y wedde myn **eyes**
145 That lawe schal be a laborer ant lede a feld donge
Ant Loue schal lede **the** as the lef lycuht."
Clerkus that were confessores coupled hem togyderes,
For to construe thys clause declined faste.
Ac to Resoun among tho r[e]nkus haued yrehersed this wordus,
150 There nas man in the mote, more ne lasse,
That ne held Mekenesse a mayster ant Mede a muche wrech,
Ant sworen be seynt Rycher a schent the rewme.
| Loue let of here ly3te, lawghed here to scorne,
| Ant seyde so lowde that Sothenese hit herde,
155 "Ho so wylneth here to wyue for welth of here godes,
But he be cokewold ykald, kutte of my nose!"
Conscyence, Cryst wot, knewe wel the sothe.
The kyng ant Resoun aryse ant reykes in to chaumbre
Ant busked to boure; Y beheld hem no lengur.

Z 141-151 = **A** 126-136; **Z** 152; **Z** 153-156 = **A** 137-140; **Z** 157-159.

141   nullum: ullum or nllum **Z** (lacking abbreviation sign).
     erit (E, after malum, but with different syntax): wiþ **A**. Published editions of
Innocent III De miseria humanae conditionis (PL 217, 745, iii, 16; ed. M. Maccarone
[Lugano, 1955], iii, 18; ed. Robert E. Lewis [Athens, Ga., 1978], iii, 14) all read nullum
malum preterit impunitum, but the line is often cited with erit (e.g., John of Bromyard, s.
Bonitas, ⁋ 11) or with no verb. We owe this information to Ms. Anne Quick, who tells us
that the line appears in works earlier than Innocent, such as Peter Lombard's commentary
on Romans (PL 191, 1341); its ultimate source was perhaps Gregory the Great (PL 76, 76).
142   And bad Nullum bonum be irremuneratum **A** (IV 127). The **Z** reading is forceful
and attractive, but syntactically awkward.
143   kenne: construe **A** (IV 128).
     on: om. **Z**.
144   dede: werk **A** (IV 129).
     eyes: eris **A**.
146   the: þi land **A** (IV 131).
149   to = tho "when" (cf. þo L). renkus: ronkus **Z**.
150   mote (W): mothalle **A** (IV 135).
151   Mekenesse (AM, **B**-text): Resoun **A** (IV 136).
152   Unique to **Z**: "and swore by Saint Richard that she (Meed) harmed the kingdom."
Rycher is presumably St. Richard of Chichester, noted for his stern stand against simony.
157-159   Unique to **Z**. Lines 158-159 conflict with what follows: see Introduction,
p. 14.

Passus Quintus

¶ Wareyn Wysdom ant Wytty ys fere
Cowthe nat warpen a word to wy*th*segge Resoun,
But stared for studiyng **as a ston stylle.**
The kyng acorded by Cryst to Resoun sawes
5 Ant seyde that Resoun ryghtfullyche haued schewed,
"Ac hit ys ful hard, by myn heued, herto to bryng*en* hit
Ant my lege led*us* to lede th*us* euene."
"By hym that raw3te on the rode," q*ua*d Resoun to the kyng,
"But Y rewle th*us* thy rewme, rend of my **heres,**
10 Yf **ye bydde** buxumesse be of myn assente."
"Ant Y assente," q*ua*d the kyng, "by seynt Mary my lady,
Be my consayl ycome of clerk*us* ant herles.
Ac redely, Resoun, thow schalt nat ryde hennes:
For as long as Y lyue, leue Y the nelle."

Z v 1-9 (cf. **Z** iv 122-130) = **A** iv 141-149; **Z** 10-14 = **A** iv 150-154.

1-8   These lines (= **A** iv 141-148) repeat **Z** iv 122-129 above: see Introduction, p. 14.

3   *But stariden for stodyenge and stoden as bestis* (etc.) **A** (iv 143), *But stoden stylle as stuty hors that dolleth* **Z** iv 124. Thus, the first half of the line is close to **A**, but the second half is found nowhere else.

4   Like **A** iv 144 rather than **Z** iv 125.

5   Like **Z** iv 126 rather than **A** iv 145.

7   *Ant: Alle* **Z** iv 128; *lede: lede hem* **Z** iv 128; all these readings have support among **A** mss.

9   Cf. **Z** iv 130, where Reason is telling the king himself how to rule; in its present position the line operates as it does in the **A**-text (iv 149), in which Reason is talking about his own rule.

heres: ribbes **A** (iv 149). Some mss of the A-text read *rend of* (instead of *rend out*), which may be a vestige of **Z**.

10   *ye bydde* (**B**): *it be þat* **A** (iv 150).

13   *ryde*: so most **A** (iv 153) and **B** mss. Kane (pp. 161-162) argues in favour of *raike*, as the *difficilior lectio*, partly to explain TDH[2] *wende*.

14   *leue* (*leuyn* A, four **B** mss): *lete* (etc.) **A** iv 154. The reading *leue*, however, is concealed in *loue* in seven **A** mss.

fol. 132v   "I am aredy," qu*a*d Resoun, "to reste w*yth* yow euere,

16   So Conscyence be of oure consayl, kepe Y no bettre."

"Ant Y graunte," qu*a*d the kyng, "God*us* forbode he fayle,

| As longe as Y lyue, libbe togyderes."

The kyng ant ys knytes to the kyrke wente

20   Tho here matynes ant masse ant to the mete aft*ur*.

Thenne waked Y of my wynkyng ant wo was w*yth* alle

That Y ne haued slepe sadd*ur* ant yseyn more.

Ar Y haued fare a forlong, fey*n*tyse me hent

That Y ne my3te forth*ur* a fot for **slep that me folwed.**

25 | Y sat softely adow, sayd **Y "by my leue,"**

Ant so Y babled on my bed*us*, they brow3te me a slepe,

| Ant say muche more then fore telle.

For Y saw the feld ful of folk that Y afore tolde,

Ant Conscience w*yth* a cros com for to preche

30   Ant preyde the peple haue pyte of hemsylue,

Ant pr*i*ued the pestilence was for puyr synne

Ant sothewoste wynd a sat*ur*day at eue

Was pertlyche for pruyde ant for no poynt elles.

For word ys but wynd ant so my wyt telleth,

35   **Ac wel Y wot that holy wryt wot muche bettre**

Z 15-18 = **A** IV 155-158; **Z** 19-33 = **A** v 1-15; **Z** 34-35.

---

18   The A-text (IV 158) has *we* after *libbe*, clarifying the syntax. In **Z** *libbe* is infinitive after *graunte* (17): "and I agree to live together (with Conscience) – God forbid (lit. God's forbidding) that he fail (to guide me)."

19   *kyrke*: on the *kirke/chirche* variation, see Kane, p. 157.

20   *Tho* "to."

24   *slep that me folwed*: *defaute of slepyng* (etc.) **A** (v 6).

25   *by my leue*: *my beleue* **A** (v 7). The "spoonerism" may be the scribe's slip or a deliberate joke by Langland (cf. *babled* 26); if the latter, it was eliminated or lost in all subsequent versions.

27   *fore telle* (*I fortelle* DL): *I before tolde* **A** (v 9). For **Z**'s sense, see MED *fore* adv. 3(c). **Z**'s line could mean "I saw much more than to speak of," but perhaps supply *I* before *fore*. Kane (p. 440) regards variants on *tolde* 27-28 (**A** v 9-10) as scribal interference to avoid the repetition.

31   *priued*: the form is paralleled in the OED, but an abbreviation error (for *preued*) is possible.

34-40   Unique to **Z**. Line 34 is a proverb: B. J. Whiting, *Proverbs, Sentences and Proverbial Phrases* (Cambridge, Mass., 1968), **W** 643. The passage, which seems very Langlandian, was perhaps cancelled as digressive or even as mildly unorthodox (cf; 37-38).

Ant wytnesseth that God*u*s word ys worthyokest of alle.

Hit maketh the messe ant the masse that men vnderfongeth

For God*u*s body ant ys blod, buyrnes to saue;

Helle yat*u*s hit tobarst ant hadde out Adam;

40   W*yth* wynd of ys word al this world made.

Ant in ensaumple, segges, that ye schal do the bettre,

Bech*u*s ant brod okes weren blowe to the erthe,

Al to warne vs weyes wat thys werd menes.

Peryes ant plomtres were poste to the erthe,

45   Assches ant helmes ant okes ful heye,

| Turne vpward here tayl yn toknyg of drede

| That dedly synne ar dom*u*s day fordo schal hem alle.

Of thys matere Y my3te mamele ful longe,

Ac Y schal seye as Y say, so me God helpe,

50   How Conscyence w*yth* ys cros cumseth to preche.

A bad Wastor to wyrche wat a beste couthe,

To wynne*n* here wastyng w*yth* su*m*me manere craft,

Ant preyd P*er*nele here porfyl to leue,

To kepe hit in here cofre Conscyence bysowte.

55   Thomme Stoue a tau3te to take to staues

Ant fette hom Felice from wyue*n* pyne;

Warned Wat ys wyf was to blame,

| That here heued was at alfmark ant ys hode at a grote.

Z 36-40; Z 41-42 = A 17-18; Z 43; Z 44 = A 16; Z 45; Z 46-58 = A 19-31.

37   "the meal and the mass."

40   Understand "he" or "who," referring to God (understood in line 39).

41 ff.   In A, 44 (A v 16) is placed before 41.

43   *werd*: "word" or "world" or "fate." At viii 174 (Q-section) *werd* is certainly "world," but *e/o* confusion is possible here (Introduction, p. 31).

44   *poste* "pushed" (shared by several A mss): *puffid* (etc.) A (v 16). The reading *puffid*, usually adopted by editors, is more striking.

46   *turne*: *And turnide* (etc.) A (v 19). Z's syntax is unclear; perhaps read *turned*.

50   *cumseth: cumside* (etc.) A (v 23).

52   *here wastyng* (*his wastyng* B): *þat he wastide* A (v 25). In Z Waster appears to be feminine, unless *here* = "their." In line 51 a^2 may be masculine or feminine.

54   *Conscyence bysowte: for catel at nede* A (v 27); the Z line is weak.

55   *Themme* cancelled before *Thomme* Z.
    Thomme Stoue (*Tomme of Stowe* J, *Tomme Stowue* B): *Thomas* A.

58   *at alfmark* (*worþ halfmark* N, C, and many B mss): *worþ a mark* (etc.) A (v 31).

A bad Bette to kytte a bow or tweye
60   **Ant bete Beden theremyde but yf he wold wyrche;**
       Charged chapmen to chasten here chyldren,
       Lat no wynnyng forwanyen hem wyle they ben yonge;
       Preyed prelatus ant prestus **yfere**
       That they prechyd the peple, preue hit in hemsylf,
65   Ant libben as they lere vs, we wyl leue hem th[e] bettre.
fol. 133r   Ant senes a radde religioun here rewle to holde,
       "Last the kyng ant his consayl youre comewnes apeyre
       Ant be styward of youre stedes tyl ye be stywed bettre.
       Ant ye that sekut seyn James ant seyntes of Rome,
70   **Jerusalem ant Jeryco ant Jacobes welle,**
       Sekut seynt Trewthe for he may saue yow alle,
       Qui cum patre et fili[o] that fayre **hem** byfalle
       That doth as Y dome wyle here dayes lasten;
       The sone wyth the seynt spiryt saue hem fro meschaunce
75   **That seweth my sarmon ant thus secuth Trewthe."**
       ¶ Thanne ran Repentaunce, rehersed ys teme,
       Ant gerte Wylle to wepe watur wyth his eyes.
       Pernele prowd-herte platte here to the erthe
       Ant lay longe ar a locud ant "lord, mercy" cryed,
80   Ant byhyght to hym that vs alle made
       A scholde vnsowen here serk ant sette there an haire,
       For to afayten here flesch that fers was to synne:
       "Schal nere heye herte me hente but holde [me] lowe

Z 59-60; **Z** 61-69 = **A** 32-40; **Z** 70; **Z** 71-72 = **A** 41-42; **Z** 73-75; **Z** 76-83 = **A** 43-50.

59-60   These lines (= **B** v 32-33, **C** vi 135-136) are also in **A** mss JEAM.

63-65   Written as two lines in **Z**, divided after *peple*.

63   *yfere: togidere* **A** (v 34).

64   *prechyd* (W): *preche* **A**. Some mss have *and* after *peple* but Kane (p. 160) argues against it.

65   *the: th* **Z**. *leue*: supported by Kane (p. 440).

70   Unique to **Z**.

72   *filio: filij* **Z**.
       hem (**C**; *hym* E): *ȝow* **A**.

73-75   73-74 are unique to **Z**, but 75 is similar to **B** v 59 (**C** vi 201), which is in mss EKWM of the **A**-text. *dome*: cf. I 31 note, above.

77   *gerte* (**A**, many **B** mss): *made* **A** (v 44).

83   *me: one* **Z** (cf. 136 note, below).

Ant suffre to be mys-seyd, ant so dide Y nere.
85　But now wyl Y meke me ant mercy byseche
　　Of alle **hem** that Y haue had enuye in myn herte."
　| Lecherye seyde "alas" ant oure ledy cryed
　　To make mercy for ys mysdede bytwene God ant ys sowle,
　| Wyth a scholde the saturday seuen yer thereaftur
90　Drynke but myt the doke ant dyne bot ones.
　　Enuye ant yre ayther wep faste,
　　Preyude furst to Pouel ant tho Petur also,
　　To geten grace for here gult of God that hem boughte,
　　That nere wyked wylle ne wrath hem ouerecome,
95　**But sende hem grace to suffre ant synne to lete**
　　Ant for to louye ant be byloued as Charite wolde.
　　Thenne com Couetyse, knoked ys brest;
　　A haued a Northfolk nose, Y noem ful god hede,
　　Ant swor by "so the yk" that synne scholde he lete
100　**Ant nere wolle to wey ne worstedes make**
　　Ne morgage manere wyth monye that he haued,
　　But "wenden to Walsingham ant my wyf alse

Z 84-90 = **A** 51-57; [om. **A** 58-141]; **Z** 91-98; **Z** 99-100 (cf. **A** 142-143); **Z** 101; **Z** 102 =
A 144.

86　*hem*: om. **A** (v 53); "Of all those of whom I have had envy."

87　**A** (and **B**) has *to* or *on* before *oure ledy* (cf. Kane, p. 440); for **Z**'s construction, see
MED *crien* 5(b).

89　*Wyth*: *wiþ þat* **A** (v 56): "provided that."

91-96　In place of these lines **A** has v 58-106, on Envy alone. See Introduction, pp. 18-
19.

94　"That wicked will and wrath should never overcome them."

97-103　The description of Covetousness is expanded in the A-text to v 107-145, by
replacing 97-98 and 101, retaining only 99-100 and 102-103.

98　On satire against Norfolk, see Introduction, pp. 16-17.

99　*Ac I swere now so thee ik þat synne wol I Lete* **B** (v 226); for *so thee ik* (written *so
theyk* in **Z**) most **A** mss have *soþly* in some form. Kane reads *so þe I* (and discusses the
sequence of corruption, p. 164), based on *so þike* N, *so mote I the* AMH[3], *als mote I the* E
(cf. J *so I think*). Thus the "Norfolk oath" (cf. *Canterbury Tales* RvT A 3864 *so theek*, used
to characterize Oswald's Norfolk dialect) is preserved in **ZB**, with traces in some **A** mss. Its
appropriateness to Covetousness is only made clear by **Z** v 98, although it has never been
questioned.

100　Worsted cloth takes its name from the Norfolk village. The implication of the
line, presumably, is not that weighing wool or making worsted cloth are in themselves
reprehensible, but that they should not be done covetously. **A** here reads: *Ne neuere
wykkidly weiʒe ne wykkide chaffare make* (**A** v 143; similarly **B**).

101　Unique to **Z**. This occurrence antedates MED *morgage* v. (see also **Z** III 96).

Ant bydde the rode of Bromholm brynge vs out of dette."
Thenne gan Gloten to grete ant gret sorwe made
105 **Al** for ys luyther lyf that a lyued hadde;
Ant a voued faste for eny hung*ur* or furste
"Schal nere fysch vpon the fryday defye*n* in my wombe
Ar Abstinence myn aunte haue yf me leue –
Ant yut hath **he hated me** al my lyf tyme."
110 Slewthe for sorw ful down y swowe
Tyl *Vigilate* **ant veyles** fette wat*ur* at ys ey*us*;
Flatted hit on ys face ant faste on hym cryed
Ant seyde "War the fro wanhope wolde the **to-traye**:
"Ych am sory of my synnes" sey to thyselue,
115| Ant bete thysylf on thy brest, bydde hym of grace
fol. 133v For his no gult here so gret that his godnesse ne his more."
| Thenne sat Slewthe vp, seyned hym faste
Ant mad[e] a vow tofore God for ys foule **synne**;
"Schall no sonenday be thys seue*n* yer, but syknesse yt make,
120 That Y ne schal do me ar day to the dere chirche
To here masse ant matynes as Y a monek were.
Schal non ale aft*ur* mete halde me thennes

Z 103 = **A** 145; [om. **A** 146-206]; **Z** 104-122 = **A** (207) 208-225.

104-109   These lines are retained in **A** (v 207-212), but are there preceded by the lengthy account of Gluttony (**A** v 146-206).

104   Cf. **A** v 207: *And gan grete grymly & gret doel m̄ake*, but **Z** is slightly closer to **B** v 379: *And þanne gan Gloton greete and gret doel to make*.

106   *faste* (W, three **B** mss): *to faste* **A** (v 209), altering the sense.
furste: for the form with *f* (also in N) see also **Z** vii 165.

109   *he hated me* (*he* = "she"): *I hatid hire* (etc.) **A** (v 212).

110-130   **A** omits **Z** 130, but otherwise the confession of Sloth is the same length in **Z** and **A** (v 213-232).

111   *ant veyles* "calls (noun) to awake": *þe veil* **A** (v 214).

113   *totraye* "torment severely": see OED *to* prefix² 2 (citation from the *Proverbs of Alfred*) + *tray* v¹ (OE *tregian*). The **A**, **B** and **C** texts all have the easier *betraye*: Langland himself may have rejected the archaic and difficult *totraye* in his revision. In **Z** 113 *trayed* could be from *traye* or *betray*, probably the latter.

114   *synnes*: Kane (p. 444) argues that sg. *synne* is the *difficilior lectio*.

116   *ger* cancelled before *gret* **Z**.

118   *made*: *mada* **Z**.
synne: *slouþe* (etc.) **A** (v 221); the **A** reading is more precise.

122   *ale*: corrected (by expunction) from *alle*.

Tyl Y haue hensong yherd, Y byhote, **wyle Y lybbe,**
†**Quod ye nan**† yelde ayey*n* yf Y so myche haue,
125   Al that Y wykedely wan senes Y wyt haued.
Thow3 me lyflode lake, leten Y nelle
Than vch man schal haue hys ar Y hennes wende,
Ant w*yth* the residue ant the remenau*n*t by the rode of Chestre
| Seke*n* seynt Trewth therew*yth* or Y se Rome
130   **Or James or Jeru*s*alem by *Jesus* of euene.**"
Robert the robbere on *reddite* locut,
Ac for **he haued** nat werew*yth* a wep swythe sore
Ac yut the synful schrewe seyde to hymsylfe:
"Cryst that vpon Caluary vpon the cros deydest,
135   Tho Dismas my brother bysow3the [the] of *g*race,
Ant hauedest m*er*cy **for his mysdedes** for *memento* **ones,**
So rewe on me, Robert, that *reddere* ne habbe
Ne nere wene to wynne w*yth* craft that Y knowe.

Z 123-129 = **A** 226-232; **Z** 130; **Z** 131-136 = **A** 233-238; **Z** 137-138 = **A** 241-242.

123   *hensong* "evensong."
   wyle Y lybbe: to þe rode **A** (v 226).

124   *Quod ye nan*: corrupt. Most **A** and **B** mss read *And 3et wile I* (etc.), but two **A** mss
(H³ and M, **A** v 227) and two **B** mss (R and F, **B** v 455) have something similar to **Z**: H³
Qwat euer I namm, M *And euerche man*, R *what I nam*, F *and what y haue take to*. F's
reading is certainly derived from one with *nam*. (1) **Z**'s reading may conceal *Qwat I nam*;
if so, *yelde* is infinitive after *byhote* (123), and **Z**'s exemplar must have had *Qu* for /wh/,
which is otherwise invariably spelled *w* (the Q-conclusion, however, regularly has *Qw*). (2)
It is also possible that Langland originally wrote *Quodque mnam* (not knowing the gender
of *mna*) "and to return every mnam....," referring to Luc 19:11-27; this would explain
euerche (M) and *euer-I* (= "every," H³).

127   *Than* (= ar than "before"): *That* **A** (v 230). The syntax of both **A** and **Z** is loose.

128-129   Divided after *remenaunt* in **Z**, but with a slash after *chestre*.

129   *seken: I wile seke* (etc.) **A** (v 232). Kane (p. 444) offers some arguments against
seynt before *Trewthe*: in **Z** it is metrically desirable, and may be vestigial in those **A** mss
which retain it.

130   Unique to **Z**.

132   *he haued* (one **B** ms): *þer was* **A** (v 234).
   þw cancelled before *swythe* **Z**.

135   *the*: probably omitted by haplography after *by sow3the*.

136   *for his mysdedes: on þat man* **A** (v 238).
   ones: sake **A**. *ones* could be an error for Latin *mei* (cf. v 83), but makes adequate
sense.

137-138   After **Z** v 140 in **A**.

137   *reddere*: supported by Kane (p. 444).

138   *knowe*: Kane (p. 444) argues for N's reading *owe*.

| | Thy wille worth vpon me, as Y wel disserued
140 | To haue helle for euere, **nere hope a that Y haue**.
     | For **youre** muchyl mercy mytygacion Y byseche,
     | **For *fodere non valeo*, so feble ar my bones:**
     | **Caucyon, ant Y couthe, *caute* wolde Y make,**
     | **That Y ne begged ne borwed ne in despeyr deyde.**"
145 | Ac wat byful of thys felown Y can nat fayre schewe;
     | Wel Y wot a wep faste water wyth ys eyes
| | Ant knowleched ys coupe yut eftsones to Cryst,
     | That *penitencia* ys pyk a **wolde** polsche newe
     | Ant lepe wyth hym oure lond al ys lyf **days**,
150 | For **that** he lay by *Latro*, Luciferes aunte.
     | A thowsend of men to throngen togydyres,
     | Wepyng ant waylyng for here mysdedes,
     | Cryend vpward to Cryst an to ys clene modur
     | Grace to go to Trewthe – God leue that a mote!
155 ¶ Ac there was **weye** [none] so wys that the way thydur couthe,
     | But blostred forth as bestes ouer baches ant hilles,
     | Tyl late ant longe that they a lede mette,
     | Yparayled as a paynym in palmeres wyse.

Z 139-140 = **A** 239-240; **Z** 141 = **A** 243; [om. **A** 244]. **Z** 142-144; **Z** 145-154 = **A** 245-254; **Z** 155-158 = **A** vi 1-4.

139   *Y: I have* **A** (v 239).

140   *nere hope a that Y haue: ʒif þat hope nere* **A** (v 240). **Z** means: "if it were not for the hope that I have"; *a* should probably be deleted, but could conceivably be an exclamation.

141   *youre: þi* **A** (v 243).

142-144   Unique to **Z** (which does not have **A** v 244). The reference is to Luc. 16:1-13 (the Unjust Steward), which explains the use of the technical term *caucyon* "surety"; the pun *caute* is Langland's own. "For I cannot dig, so feeble are my bones. If I could, I would prudently make a down payment, in order not to beg or borrow or die in despair." The lines seem characteristically Langlandian; for the alliteration of /f/ and /v/, cf. **B** xv 61.

148   *wolde* (**C**): *shulde* **A** (v 248).

149   *days: tyme* **A** (v 249).

150   *that he lay: he hadde leiʒe* (etc.) **A** (v 250).

151   *to throngen: to* could be the prefix or = *tho* "when" (as in **A**).

152   *mysdedes* (H): *wykkide dedis* **A** (v 252).

154   *grace* (**A**, one **B** ms): *to haue grace* **A** (v 254).

155   Here **A** begins Passus vi: **Z** has a paragraph mark.
      weye none (**C**, *wiʒt noon* **B**): *weye* **Z**: *fewe men* (etc.) **A** (vi 1).
      there cancelled after *wys* **Z**.

156   *baches* (W, **C**): *valeis/dales/bankes* **A** (vi 2); Kane (p. 444) argues for, and adopts, *baches*.

158   *palmeres* (W): *pilgrimys* **A** (vi 4).

A bar a bordoun ybounde w*yth* a brode lyste,
160   In a **wethewyse** ywowden aboute,
A bagge ant a bolle he bar by ys syde,
An hendret of haumpelles on ys hatte setu*n*,
Sygnes of Syse ant schelles of Galis
Ant many a crowche on ys clok ant keyes of Rome,
165   Ant the v*er*nycle afore, for me*n* scholde yknowe
Ant se be ys signes wam a sowght adde.

Z 159-166 = **A** vi 5-12.

160   *wethewyse*: various spellings are found in the mss: see Kane, p. 444.
162   *an hendret* (one word in **Z**) "one hundred"; on *e* for /u/, see Appendix, p. 121.
163   *Syse* (M, one **B** ms, **C**, *asyce* A): *Synay* (etc.) **A** (vi 9); "Assisi."
165-166   Written as prose in **Z**, divided after *wam*; this is the bottom of the page.

Passus Sextus

fol. 134r   This folk frayned hym furst fro wannes a come.
        "Fram Synay," a sayde, "ant fro the sepulcre of oure lord;
| Bedleh[e]m ant Babelonye Y haue **ysougwth** bothe,
        In Ermonye, in Alisaundre, in many oth*ur* plases.
    5 Ye mowe*n* se by my sygnes that sitteh[t] on my hatte
        That Y haue walked ful wyde in wete ant in drye
        Ant sought gode seynt*us* for my sowle hele."
        "**Ac** knowest thow hau3t a corseynt that men calleth Trewthe?
        Cowthest wissen vs the wey there the weye dwelleth?
   10 "Nay, so me God helpe," seyth the gome thenne,
        "Y say nere palmare **myt** pyk ne w*yth* scrippe
        Axen aft*ur* hym ar now in this place."
        "Pet*ur* !" *qua*d a plow[e]man ant potte forth his heued.
        "Y knowe hym as kyndely as clerk doth ys boc*us*:
  15 | Conscyence kened me to his place,
        Ant **senes Y suyred** hym to serue hym for euere,
        Bothe to sowe ant to sette wyle Y swynke myghte.
        I haue ben ys folwaere al this fourty wynt*ur*,
    | Bothe ysowen ys seed, sewed his best*us*,
  20 Ant eke ykept ys corn, ycaryed hit to howse,

Z vi 1-20 = **A** vi 13-32.

   1   *furst* (H³ (*fryst*), all **B** mss except F (om.), **C**): *fast/faire* **A** (vi 13).
   3   *ysougwth: ben* in **A** (vi 15). *Bedlehem: Bedlehom* **Z**.
   5   *sitteht: sitteh* **Z**.
   9   *cowthest* (*Koudestow* many **B** mss, **C**): *canst þou* (etc.) **A** (vi 21).
  10   *gome*: supported by Kane (p. 444).
  11   *myt: wiþ* **A** (vi 23).
  13   *ploweman: plowo man* **Z**.
  15   The line is too short; a reading such as N (**A** vi 27) and **B** *Conscience and kynd wyt*
(cf. W *Conscience and clene witte*) would be appropriate, and the omission of *and kynd
wyt* would be explained by haplography of *kynd/kened*. Cf. **A**: *Clene* (*kynde* H) *consience
& (*om. H) *wyt* (*kynd wyt* H² [*kynd* cancelled], om. H) *kende/tau3te me to his place*, etc.
  16   *senes Y suyred* "afterwards I assured": *dede me sure* **A** (vi 28).

Ydyked ant ydolue, do that a highte,
Both wy*th*inne ant wy*th*outen ywayted ys p*r*ofit.
There ys no laborer in this lordschepe that a loueth bettre,
For thow Y sey hit mysilf, Y serue hym to paye.
25 Y haue myn huyre of hym wel ant oth*ur*wyle more;
He ys the p*r*estest payere that pore men yknoweth.
He wy*th*halt noen hew ys huyre that he ne hath hit at eue.
He ys as low as a lomb ant loueli*ch*e of speche.
Yf ye wilneth to wyte were **this** weye dwelleth,
30 | Y schal wisse yow the way wel ryght to ys place."
¶ "Ye, leue P*er*es," q*u*od the pileg*r*imes ant p*r*ofred hym huyre.
| "Nay," **q*u*ad P[er]kyn the plowman**, "by the p*er*el of my sowle,
I nolde nat fong a ferthyng for seynt Thomas schryne:
Trewthe wold loue me the wers a long tyme aft*ur*.
35 Ac ye wilne to wende, this ys the wey thed*ur*e.
Ye mote*n* go thorw Mekenesse, bothe men ant wyues,
Tyl [ye] come into Conscyencie, Cryst wot the sothe,
That [ye] loueye*n* hym leuere than your*e* oune hert*u*s,
Ant your*e* neyhebores nexst in none wyse apeyre
40 Oth*ur* wyse than thow wo[l]t a wroughte to thysilf.
Ant so boweth by a brok, Beth-buxum **ys called**,

Z 21-41 = **A** 33-53.

22 *Bothe* (W): om. **A** (vɪ 34).

27 *hew* (N, most **B** mss, **C**): *hyne* **A** (vɪ 39).

29 *weye*: supported by Kane (p. 445).

30 The word order differs from that of **A** mss (discussed by Kane, p. 445): the **Z** reading provides a good basis to explain the **A** readings.

32 Most **A** mss (vɪ 44) have *quaþ piers* and place it after *soule*; they all have *and gan to swere* (etc.) at the end of the line. *Perkyn*: *Pkyn* **Z**.

34 Apart from the omission of *For* (omitted by many **A** mss), **Z**'s line agrees with that printed (from T) by Kane as the one most likely to be a source of error in the other mss (Kane, p. 445).

35 Perhaps read *Ant* for *Ac*, or supply *yf*.

37 *ye*: om. **Z**.

38 *ye*: om. **Z**.
    youre oune hertus (E): *þe lif in ʒoure hertis* **A** (vɪ 50).

40 *wolt*: *wost* **Z** (and J!): *woldist* **A** (vɪ 52). The emendation is essential: Piers is hardly likely to say "only harm your neighbours in the way you know they did to you." *l* and *s* are easily confused.
    a "he": note the change of number from 39.

41 *ys called*: *of speche* **A** (vɪ 53).

Forto ye fynden a ford Youre-faderes-anhoureth.

Wadeth in **at** that wat*ur* ant wassche yow wel there

Ant ye schal **lyue the leng*ur* by a long** tyme.

45   So schalt thow se Swere-nat-but-yf-yt-be-for-nede

Ant-namlyche-an-ydel-the-name-of-**oure-lorde**

Ant Holde-so-the-alyday-heye-tyl-eue.

Thenne schat þow come by a croft, but come þow nat th*er*einne:

The croft hatteth Coueyte-nat-mennes-catel-ne-wyues.

50 | Brek **nat a** bow therof but yf hit be thyn oune.

fol. 134v   To stokk*us* there standeth, **ac** stinte þow nat there:

They hatte Stele-nat-ne-sle-nat; stryk forth by bothe,

Lef hem on thy lift hond ant loke nat thereaft*ur*.

Thenne schalt thow blenche at a berew Bere-no-false-wytnesse,

55 | Ys frethyd in w*yth* florynes ant other feus monye:

  | Ploke thow plonte there for p*er*el of thy soule!

Thenne schalt thow se Sey-soth-so-it-be-to-done-

Ac-in-no-manere-elles-nat-for-no-mannes-bydding.

Thenne schalt þow come to a court as clere as the sonne:

60   The mote ys of m*er*cy the man*er*e aboute,

  | Ant alle the walles of wyt to holde*n* wel throute.

The carneles ben of **confort, crysten*men*** to saue,

Z 42-46 = A54-58; Z 47 = A 66; Z 48-49 = A 59-60; [om. A 61]; Z 50-53 = A 62-65;
Z 54-62 = A 67-75.

42   *Forto*: supported by Kane (p. 445).

44   **Z**'s very feeble line is replaced in **A** (vɪ 56) by the much more vigorous *And ʒe
shuln lepe þe liʒtliere al ʒoure lif tyme.*

46   *oure lord*: god almiʒt (etc.) **A** (vɪ 58).

47   Placed after **Z** 53 in **A** (vɪ 66). The placing of this commandment in **Z**, immediately
after "Swear not," is closer to the traditional order, but, as Bennett notes (on **B** v 570 ff.)
Langland does not give a complete resumé of the Ten Commandments; even in **Z** the
order is not biblical.

49   After this line **A** has vɪ 61 (om. ᴍꜱ A).

50   *Brek nat a bow*: Loke þou breke no bowis (bowe) (etc.) **A** (vɪ 62).

51   *ac* (**BC**): but **A** (vɪ 63).

54   *berew*: supported by Kane (p. 445).

55   *frethyd*: supported by Kane (p. 445).

56   *Ploke thow plonte*: (*And*) Loke þou plukke no plante **A** (vɪ 69). **Z** may mean: "You
pluck a plant there at the risk of your soul," but probably supply *no*.

61   *walles*: wallis ben (etc.) **A** (vɪ 74).

    wel (UE): wil **A** (vɪ 74); cf. **Z** ɪv 20, where **Z** has the personification and **A** has *wel*. In
the present line in **Z**, holden is intransitive (see ᴍᴇᴅ *holden* v (1) 22-24).

62   *confort crystenmen*: cristendom þat kynde **A** (vɪ 75).

Ant bot*ur*ased w*yth* **baptewme to brynge me*n* to heuen*e*.
Alle the hous ben yheled, halles ant chaumbres,
65   W*yth* no led but w*yth* loue **that longeth to the place.**
The toure there Trwthe ys hymsylf **tyleth** vp to the sonne.
A **doth** w*yth* the day sterre that hym dere licuth:
A may se in the mone wat all*e* men thenketh.
W*yth* the lest word that a wil, the wynd ys aredy
70   **To blowe or to be stille or to brethy softe,**
Ant alle the water of thys world wolde in his gloue.
He hath fuyr w*yth*oute*n* flint ys foes to brenne.
Deth dar nat do thyng that he defendeth.
The forst for fere ys fayn to folwen ys wille.
75   **Dar no st*ere* steren hym ne steme ayeyn ys defense.**
I haue no tome to telle how the tour ys ymaked:
Alle the wryght*us* at Wyndelesore couthe wirche such an oth*ur*
Ne alle the masounes of this lound make there a spanne.
The bryge hatte Byde-wel-the-bet-may-the-spede.
80   **Vch piler ys of penaunse, ypolsched ful smethe.**
Grace hatte the gateward, a god man for s[o]the;

Z 63-67 = **A** 76-80; **Z** 68-72; **Z** 73 = **A** 81; **Z** 74-80; **Z** 81 = **A** 82.

63   *baptewme ... heuene: beleue so oþer þou best not sauid* **A** (vi 76).

64   *hous* (plural): *housis* (etc.) **A** (vi 77).

65   *that ... place:* *& louȝnesse as breþeren of o wombe* (etc.) **A** (vi 78).

66   *tyleth: is* **A** (vi 79), lacking alliteration. *tyleth* "extends": see OED *till* v.²; cf. **C**-text vii 220.

67   *doth: may do* **A** (vii 80).

68-75   These lines on the powers of Truth are omitted in **A**, except for 73 (which is omitted in **B** and **C**). "He may see in the moon what all men think. At the slightest word that he wishes, the wind is ready to blow or be still or breathe softly, and all the water of the world would fit in his glove. He has fire without flint, to burn his foes.... The frost, for fear, is eager to follow his will. No star dare stir (steer?) itself nor stop (contend) against his command." For *steme* 75, see OED *stem* v² 1 and v³.

76-78   Unique to **Z**.

77   Major new building began at Windsor in 1354 (Walsingham, *Historia Anglicana*, i, 288, cited by L. F. Salzman, *Building in England down to 1450* [Oxford, 1952]) and continued throughout the fourteenth and fifteenth centuries: Chaucer was supervisor in 1388-1389. For an account of the large numbers of masons and bricklayers in 1365, see Salzman, p. 60.
    A negative is understood, or has been inadvertently omitted.

79-80   = **B** v 592-593, **C** viii 240-241; also in **A** MSS EAMH³, where they follow **Z** 73.

80   *ypolsched ful smethe: of preieres to seyntes* **B** (v 593) **C** (viii 241).

81   *sothe: sethe* **Z**.

His man hatted Amende-yow; many man hym knoweth.
Telleth hym this tokene: "Trewthe wot the sothe:
Y parformed the penawnce the preste me enioynd;
85| Am ful sory **of** my synnes ant so schal Y euere
Wen Y thenke thereon, thow3 Y were a pope.'
Byddeth Amende-yow meken hym to ys mayster
Onus to wayuen vp the wycat that the **wenche** schutte
Tho Adam ant Eue heten ere bane.
90 For he hath the keye ant the clycat, thow the kyng slepe,
Ant hif Grace graunte the to go in this wyse,
Thou schalt yse Trewthe hymsylf, wolle sitten in thyn herte
Ant leren the for to loue ant ys lawe holde.
Ac be ywar thenne of Wrath-the-nat, that wyked schrewe,
95 For he hath enuye tho hym that in thyn herte sitteth,
Ant poketh forth pruyde to preyse thyselue.
The boldenesse of thy benfetus maketh the blynd thenne,
| Ant so wo[r]st thow dryue out as deugh ant dore yclosed,
Ykayed ant yclecaked to kepe the wythouten,
100 Ant happely an hundret wyntur ar th[ou] efft entre.
fol. 135r   Thus mygh t thow lesen ys loue **in loking of a wenche,**
Ac geten hit ayeyn thorw grace **ac** thorw no gyft elles."

Z 82-102 = **A** 83-103; [om. **A** 104-123].

82   *hatted*: pr. 3 sg.
88   *Onus*: at the end of **Z** 87 in **A** (vi 88).
     wenche (*woman* **B**): *wy/wi3t* **A**. Kane (pp. 445-446) conjectures *wyf*, with arguments which operate even more strongly in favour of *wenche*.
92   *wolle* (*wil* DJ): *wel*/om. **A** (vi 93).
93   Some mss read *hym* after *loue* but Kane (p. 160) rejects it.
94   *wrath the nat*: several **A** mss (vi 95) read something similar, with the negative, but most have the noun *wrappe*. The **Z** reading is much more in Langland's manner in this passage, where the pilgrims are told to shun the negative Commandments. The reflexive verb *wrath the* (see OED *wrath* v. 3) may be concealed in *wrappe* (many **A** and **B** mss).
95   *tho* "to."
96   *poketh forth pruyde*: supported by Kane (p. 446).
98   *worst*: *woest* (?) **Z**.
99   *yclecaked* or *ycletaked*: several scribes of **A** seem to have had trouble with this word: *yclekated* would be expected.
100 *thou*: *the* **Z**.
101 *in ... wenche*: *to lete wel be piselue* **A** (vi 102).
102 *ac*[1]: *And/Bote* **A** (vi 103); *ac*[2] (**BC**, om. W): *&* **A**.
     After this line **A** adds vi 104-123 on the Seven Sisters that serve Truth.

Passus Septimus

"Thys were a wel wyked wey, but wo haued a gyde
That myght folew vs vch foet forto we were there."
Q*ua*d P*er*kyn the plowman, "Be seynt Poule **of Rome**,
Y haue an halue aker to ere by the heye way.

5   Haued Y hered that haluac*ur* ant ysowed hit aft*ur*,
†**Ant schal** wende w*yth* yow tyl **the heye weye**."
"This were a long lettyng," q*ua*d a lady in a sclayre;
"Wat scholde we wymme*n* wirch*e* the wyle?"
"So*m*me schal sowe*n* the sak for schedyng of the wete,

10   Ant wyues that han wolle*n*, wirche*n* hit faste
Ant spynneth hit spedlych, sparet nat youre fingres
But y[t] be eny halyday or eny holy eue.
Loketh forth youre lynne*n* ant laboreth thereon faste.
The nedy ant the naked, nymeth hede how he ligeth:

15   Casteth hem clothes for cold, for so comawndeth Trewthe.
For Y schal lene hem liflode, but yf the lond fayle,
As longe as Y liue, for our*e* lord*us* loue of heuene.
Ant ye louelyche ladius w*yth* youre longe fingres,

Z VII 1-18 = **A** VII 1-18.

2   *forto*: see on **Z** VI 42 above.

3   *Poule of Rome (Peter of Rome* **BC**): *Poule þe apostel* **A** (VII 3).

5   *ant ... aftur* (EAMH³, **B**, **C**): *so me god helpe* TChH²: om. remaining **A** MSS (VII 5) (and Kane). Kane (p. 446) rejects readings which complete the line after *haluacur*, on the grounds that they do not explain the omission from the other MSS.

6   *Ant schal*: *I wolde* (etc.) **A** (VII 6).

    the heye weye: *ȝe were þere* (etc.) **A**. **A** readings differ considerably for the whole line. It would be simple to emend **Z** *Ant schal* to *I schal* or *I scholde*, but the phrase *the heye weye* looks like dittography from line 4, and the whole line may be corrupt. It is possible that lines 5-6 are in draft form, and that incomplete revision explains the divergences among **A** MSS and the deficient line 5.

12   *yt*: *yf* **Z** (alternatively, read *yf yt*).

That ye haue selk ant sendel to sewen wan tyme ys,
20 Chesibles for chapeleynes chirches to honoure.
Ant al manere men that by the mete libbeth,
Helpeth hym wirche wytliche that wynneth youre fode."
¶   "By Crist," quad a knyght tho, "thow kennest vs the best,
Ac on the teme trewly taught was Y nere.
25 Ac kenne me," quad the knyght, "ant **be Cryst Y wyl lere.**"
"By seynt Petur," quad Perkyn, "an for thow profrest the so lowe,
Y schal swynken ant swete ant sowe for vs bothe,
Ant eke laboure for youre loue al my lif tyme,
In couenaunt that ye kepe holy kyrke ant mysylf
30 Fro wastors ant wyked men that wolden me destruye;
Meyntene me yf þow mygth fro al manere schrewes
Ant go hunte hardely the hares ant the foxus,
| The bukkes ant bores that breken myn egges,
Ant feteth hom faukones fowles to kulle.
35 For these cometh [to my] croft ant croppeth my wete."
Cortesliche the knyghte thenne comseth thes wordes:
"By my pouer, Peres, Y plyȝte the my trewthe
To fulfelle this forward **for euere more hereaftur.**"
"Ye, ant yut a poynt," quad Perkyn, "Y prey the, more:
40 Loke thow tene no tenaunt but **yf** Trewthe wyl assente,
Ant thouȝ pore men profre yow presauntus ant yftus,
Nyme nat, an awntre thow mow hit nat desserue.
| **Thenne** schalt thow yelden hit ayeyen at one yeres ende,

---

Z 19-30 = **A** 19-30; **Z** 31; **Z** 32-43 = **A** 31-42.

---

19   *That ye* (**B**): *þat* or *ȝe* **A** (vii 19). Some **A** mss have *to sewen* (etc.), as **Z**, but most have forms of the imperative (*sewiþ*, etc.). For the construction in **Z**, see OED *that* conj. ii 3 c, and Appendix, p. 125.

22   *wytliche*: probably = *wyghtliche* "boldly/quickly" rather than "wisely."

25   *be Cryst Y wyl lere* (*I wile fayn lern* **W**, *by crist I wole assaye* **B**): *I wile conne eren* (etc.) **A** (vii 25).

31   Unique to **Z**.

33   *bukkes ant bores*: reversed in **A** (vii 32).

35   *to my*: om. **Z**.

36   *comseth*: Kane (p. 446) argues strongly for *conseyuede*.

38   *for ... hereaftur*: *whiles I may stande* **A** (vii 37).

42   *an awntre*: *a nawntre* **Z**.

43   *Thenne schalt thow*: *For þou schalt* **A** (vii 42).

In a ful perilouse place, that Purgatorie hette.

45   Amys bed nat thy bondmen, the bet schat thow spede.
     Loke thow be trewe of thy tunge ant tales that thow hate,

fol. 135v   But yf yt be of wysdom or wyt, thy werkmen to chaste.
     Yf none harlotes thyn hode ne thyn holde clothys,
     But hit be mynstrales or messageres that gode murthes cunne."

50   "I assente, by seynt Jame," quad the knyght thenne,
     "For to wyrche by thy word wyle my lyf duyreth."
     Perkyn aparayled hym in pylgrimes wyse;
     A caste on his clothes yclouted **for the colde,**
     Ys cokeres ant ys coffus for **clumse of ys fyngres,**

55   "**Ant myn hatte on myn heued, Y haue no bettre scrippe:**
     A boschel of bred-corn bryng me thereinne,
     For Y wil sowe hit mysilf ant senes wil Y wend,
     Ant ho so helpeth me to **holde or eggen hit myt the harwe**
     Or wit awey the fowles wyle the sed grouth

60   Schal haue leue by oure lord **to lese** here in heruest
     Ant beren hit forth to his bern as baldely as mysilf."

Z 44-47 = **A** 43-46; [om. **A** 47-49]; **Z** 48-49; **Z** 50-52 = **A** 50-52; [om. **A** 53]; **Z** 53-58 = **A** 54-55 (56) 57-59; **Z** 59; **Z** 60 = **A** 60; [om. **A** 61-69]; **Z** 61.

45   *Amys bed*: (*And*) *mysbede* **A** (vii 44).

46   *Loke* (one **B** ms): *And þat* / om. (etc.) **A** (vii 45).

48-49   Unique to **Z**; replaced by **A** vii 47-49.

49   Cf. **Z** Pr 34.

52   This line (**A** vii 52) and **A** vii 53 (not in **Z**) are spoken by Piers in the **A**-text: "*And I shal apparaille me ...* etc."

53   *for the colde: and hole* **A** (vii 54).

54   *clumse ... fyngres: cold of his nailes* **A** (vii 55). For *for* + adjective, see Mustanoja, pp. 381-382; this occurrence antedates OED's citations for *clumse* (1611) and *clumsy* (1600), but Langland uses the verb (**B**-text xiv 52).

55   *And heng his hoper at his hals in stede of a scrippe* (etc.) **A** (vii 56): in **Z** Piers uses his hat to carry seed; in **A** and **B** he simply carries the hopper round his neck.

58   *holde ... harwe: eren or any þing swynke* (etc.) **A** (vii 59). **Z** means: "and whoever helps me to hold (the seed) or to harrow it (i.e., cover it over) with the harrow." For *eggen* "harrow" (used in the **C**-text, vi 19, meaning unclear), see MED v. (3), OED *edge* v².

59   Unique to **Z**: "or drive away the birds while the seeds grow." The meaning of *wit* is clear from the context: it is probably an extended sense of *wite* v² "defend, protect" (cf. the development of *ward [off]*).

60   *leue ... to lese here* (**B** vi 66, with var. *lacche* (etc.) for *lese*): *leue ... to leuyn here* MH³: ... *þe more here/hire* (etc.) **A** (vii 60). The **ZB** reading is almost certainly correct (*lese* "glean"): Kane suggests it (pp. 446-447), but does not adopt it into the text. The sequence of corruption in **A** mss ("have leave to live here," "have the more here," "have the more hire") is not easy to discern.

61   Unique to **Z**. At this point **A** has vii 61-69.

Dame Wyrche-wen-tyme-ys P*ers* wyf highte,

Ant ys dowght*ur* hyght Do-ryt-so-or-thy-dame-schal-the-bete;

Ys sone hyght "Sewe-myn-o*u*rf-fors,-slewth-nat-the-leste,

65   **Kepe vch mannes corn as thow kepest myn oune,**

Bothe here gras ant here god, or by God thow schalt abegge!

Lat nat thyne handus be yhoked harneys to pyke,

Ne ly nat to do me lawghe, for Y louede hit nere.

For now Y am hold ant hor and haue of myn owne,

70   To penaunce **as a pylgrime** Y wyl passe w*yth* this other.

Therefor Y wyl, or Y wend, do wryte my byqueste:

In dei nomine, amen: Y make hit mysylf.

He schal haue my sowle tha[t] beste hath deserued,

Ant defenden hit fro the fend, for so Y byleue,

75   Tyl **he come ant acounte,** as my crede telleth,

At dom*us* day to do me dwelle w*yth* my sowle in his blisse,

For that Y labored in ys lawe al my lyf tyme.

The kyrke schal haue my caroyne ant kepe my bones,

For of my catel ant my corn a craued my tyth.

Z 62-64 = **A** 70-71(72); [om. **A** 73-74]; **Z** 65; **Z** 66 (cf. **A** 73); **Z** 67-68; **Z** 69-75 = **A** 75-81; [om. **A** 82]; **Z** 76-77; **Z** 78-79 = **A** 83-84.

64-68   Unique to **Z**, replaced in **A** by vii 72-74.

64-65   "His son was called: 'Follow my oxen tracks, don't neglect the least of them, keep each man's corn...'"; *ourf* "cattle" (OED *orf*), *fors* "tracks, i.e., plough-furrows" (MED *fore*, senses 2 and 3), *slewthe* v. "neglect" (OED *sleuth* v[1]). (Or, with similar sense, take *forsslewth* as the compound verb "neglect".) The name of Piers' son differs entirely in **A** and **B**. In all versions, as Professor Burrow has shown, the names of Piers' family take the form of direct commands by Piers to them (J. A. Burrow, *English Verse 1300-1500* [London and New York, 1977], p. 111, notes to **B** vi 80 and 83). Thus, the direct speech begins with the name of Piers' son: in **A** and **B** it runs on into 69 (= **A** vii 75 *For now I am old*); here in **Z** it runs into 65. We are most grateful to Professor Burrow for advice on this line.

67   *harneys to pyke*: see **B** xx 263 *Pykeharneys*, OED *pick-* in comb. The phrase, originally meaning "plunder (on the field of battle)," has come to mean simply "rob."

68   Repeats **Z** iv 18, *Tomme Trewe-tong*'s name, also in **BC**.

70   *as a pylgrime: and to pilgrimage* (etc.) **A** (vii 76).

73   *that: tha* **Z**.

75   *he ... acounte: I come to his acountes* **A** (vii 81). In **Z** *acounte* means "make the reckoning": God is the auditor.

     telleth (V, many **B** MSS, **C**): *techiþ* **A**.

76-77   Unique to **Z**: replaced in **A** by vii 82, which maintains the image of rendering accounts: *To haue reles & remissioun on þat rental I leue.*

79   *catel ... corn* (H): reversed in **A** (vii 84).

     a "he," the Church: cf. *hym* 80.

80   Y payed hit hym prestly for perel of my sowle,
     Ant he his holdyng, Y hope, to haue me in his masse
     Ant menege in his memorie among **gode sowles.**
     My wyf schal haue that Y wan wyth trewthe ant no more,
     Ant dele among my **dowtres** ant my dere chyldren.
85   For thow Y deye today, my dette ys yquited:
     I bar hom that Y borwed ar Y to bedde yede.
     Ant wyth the residewe ant the remanaunt **that ryghtfullyche Y wonne**
     Y wil wirschepe therewyth Trewthe **as long as Y leue,**
     Ant be ys pilegrym at the plow for pore mens sake.
90   My plowpote schal be my pik to pich **ato** the rotus
     That acumbren my colter as cammokes ant wedus."
¶   Now ys Perkyn ant the pylegrimes to the plow faren,
     To heryen this haluacur holpen hym monye;
     Dicares ant deluares diged vp the balcus.
95   Therewyth was Perkyn apayd ant preysed hem faste.
     Othur workmen there were that wrought ful yerne,
fol. 136r   Vche man in his manere made hymsilf to done,
     For to plese Perkyn **peynd ful monye.**

Z 80-90 = **A** 85-95; [om. **A** 96]; **Z** 91; **Z** 92-98 = **A** 97-103.

---

81   *holdyng* (**C**): *holden* **A** (vii 86). See OED *beholding* pple., MED *biholden 5, holden* 14b
(a) and (b); neither MED nor OED mention the **C**-text reading. The ending *-ing*, recorded
only for *beholding* (and that only from the fifteenth century on) is explained by OED and by
Skeat (2: 109, on **C** ix 103) as a misunderstanding of final *-yn* of the pt. pp. On the other
hand, it may be a passive participle: cf. Mustanoja, pp. 548-549 and the sense "stick," MED
holden 5(a).
82   *menege* "remember."
     gode sowles: alle cristene **A** (vii 87).
84   *dowtres* (all **B** MSS, **C**): *frendis* **A** (vii 89).
87   *that ... wonne: be þe rode of Chestre* **A** (vii 92).
88   *as ... leue: in my lyue* (etc.) **A** (vii 93).
90   *plowpote, pik:* supported by Kane (p. 447).
     pich ato "pick in two, split"; *pich* (or *pick*) is in several **A** and **B** MSS; *atwo* is the
reading of most **B** MSS, but **A** readings include only *at* or *to*. Kane, therefore (p. 447),
argues in favour of *putte at.* The **Z** spelling *ato*, however, explains the **A** variants *at* and *to*,
which would have necessitated rewriting the line.
91   Unique to **Z**. Replaced in **A** by vii 96.
     cammokes: cf. **B** xix 312 (**C** xxii 314) "rest-harrow."
94   *diged:* supported by Kane (p. 447).
95-96   *faste ... yerne* (W, most **B** MSS, **C** ʒurne 96 only): reversed in **A** (vii 101-102).
98   *For to* (H³): *And summe to* **A**.
     peynd ful monye: pykide vp þe wedis (etc.) **A** (vii 103).

At heye pryme Peres let the plowe stande
100   Ant ouresey hem hymsilf: ho so best wrought
Scholde ben huyred thereaftur wen heruest tyme come.
Thenne setten summe ant songen at the nale,
Ant holpen erye the haluacur wyth "hey trolylolly."
"By the prynse of paradis," quad Peres in **his** wrath,
105   "But ye aryse the rather ant rapen yow to wirch,
Schal no grayn that here grouth gladyen yow at nede,
Ne Y nel lene yow no lyflode, noythur loef ne cake,
Ne no skines corn, by Cryst, that in my croft groueth.
Ant thow ye deye for deul, the deuel haue that reche !"
110| Thenne were faytores aferd, fayned hem blynde;
Summe leyde here leggus alyry as such loseles conneth,
Ant pleyneden to Peres wyth suche pitouse wordes:
"We han no limus to labore wyth, lord ygraced be the,
Ac we preyen for yow, Peres, ant for youre plow **also,**
115   That God for ys grace youre grayn multeplye,
Ant yelde yow oure almesse that ye yeuen vs here;
For we mowe neythur swinke ne swete, such sikenesse vs eyleth."
"3yf hit be soth that ye seyen, Y schal sone aspye.
Ye ben wastores, Y wot wyl, Trewthe wot the sothe,
120   Ant Y am his holde hyne ant houghte hym to warne
Wiche wastores in world ys werkmen distruyeth.
Ye eten that they scholde ete that eryeth for vs alle.
Ac Trewthe schal thechen yow ys teme for to dryue,
Bothe to sette ant to sowe ant to sauen ys tylthe,
125   Cach koes fro ys corn, kepen ys bestus,
Or ye schal eten barly bred ant of the brok drynke,

Z 99-106 = A 104-111; Z 107-108; Z 109-126 = A 112-129.

104   *in his wrath*: *þo in wrappe* A (vii 109).

107-108   Unique to Z; perhaps cancelled in A because of their repetitiveness.

109   *deul* "sorrow."

113   *be the*: one word in Z, but the subjunctive is essential. The construction *ygraced be* + dat. is also found in A mss UN and B mss WHm; the reading *ygraced* is supported by Kane (pp. 101, 448).

114   *also*: *boþe* A (vii 117).

120   *holde*: supported by Kane (p. 448); in Z's orthography, however, it could be "loyal" or "old."

125   *koes*: supported by Kane (p. 448). The spelling is odd.

     | But yf he blynd or broke-schanked or bedreden ligge –
      They schal ete as gode as Y, so me God helpe,
      Tyl God of ys grace gere hem to ryse.
130 Hancres ant hermytus that holdeth hem in here selles
      Schal haue of myn almesse al the wyle Y libbe,
      Ynow vch day at noen ant no more aftur,
      Laste his flesch ant the feend fouled ys sowle.
      Ones at noen ys ynow that no werk ne **haunteth**:
135 A byt wel the bettre that bummeth nat ofte."
  ¶ Thenne gan Wastor **to wrathen hym** ant wolde haue yfoughte,
   | Ant to Perus the plowman profred ys gloue.
      A Bretoner, a bragger, a bosted hym alse,
      Ant bad hym go pysse **myd** ys plowe: " **Pyuysche** schrewe,
140 Wolle þow, nelle þow, we wille han oure wille,
      Ant **bothe** thy flour ant thy flesch fech wen vs licuth,
      Ant maken vs merye theremyt mawgre thy checus."
      Thenne Peres the plowman pleyned hym to the knyghte
fol. 136v To kepen hym, as couenaunt was, fro cursed schrewes,
145 Fro wastores that wayten wynnares to schende.
      Corteslyche the knyghte thenne, as ys kynde wolde,
      Warned Wastor ant wyssed hym bettre,
      "Or thow schalt abigge by the lawe, by the ordre tha[t] Y welde."
      "I was nat woned to wirche, now wil Y nat bygynne."

Z 127-149 = **A** 130-152.

127-128 Cf. **Z** vii 197-201 below.

127 **A** and **B** (except ms R) have *be* after *he*, perhaps correctly: the vb. *ligge* may suffice for the whole line, but there is no reason why the blind should be lying down.

132 *aftur* (N): *til on þe morewe* **A** (vii 135).

133 *fouled* = *fouleth*.

134 *haunteth*: *vsiþ* **A** (vii 137).

135 *A byt* "he begs."

136 *to wrathen hym* (**BC**): *to arise* **A** (vii 139).

138 *a bosted*: seven **A** mss read *a*; Kane (p. 448) argues against a compound *abosten*, but in **Z** (and perhaps in the **A** mss) *a* = "he."

139 *myd*: *wiþ* **A** (vii 142).

     pyuysche "peevish" (**C**): *pilide* (*pyned* MH³) **A** (vii 142). Kane-Donaldson adopt *pyuysshe* for the B-text.

141 *Ant bothe* (*Bothe* **C**): *Of* (*And of* KM) **A** (vii 144).

147 *ant*: *ant ant* **Z**.

148 *that*: *thay* **Z**.

149 *now* (N): *quaþ wastour now* **A** (vii 152).

150   Ant let lighte of the lawe ant lasse of the knyght,
       Ant counted Peres at a pese ant ys plow bothe
       Ant manesed hym ant ys men **to mysdon hym eftsones.**
    ¶ | "Now by the perel of my sowle, Y schal apeyre yow alle!"
       Ant houped aftur Hungur that herd hym at the furste.
155   "Awrek me of thys wastores," quad Perus, "that this world
          schenden."
       Hungur in haste thenne hente Wastor by the mawe
       Ant wrong hym so by the wombe that al watred his eyeus,
       Ant buffated the Bretoner aboute the checus
       That a loked lik a lanterne al ys lyf aftur.
160   He bete hem so bothe that he barst nere here **guttus,**
       Ne hadde Perus wyth a pese lof preyed hym byleue.
       And wyth a beneen **botte** a yede hem bytwene,
       Ant hitte Hungur theremyde **that alle ys gottes swolle**
       Ant bledde into the bodyward a bolle ful of growel.
165   Ne hadde **sire** Furst the fycyan yfet watur **the sannure**
       To abate the barly bred ant benes **that they eten,**
       They haued be ded be thys day ant doluen al warme.
       Faytores for fere tho flowen into bernus
       Ant flapten on wyth fleyles fro morwen tyl euen
170   **Betynge barly benus ant wete,**
       That Hungur was nat hardy on hem for to loke.

Z 150-169 = **A** 153-172; **Z** 170; **Z** 171 = **A** 173.

152   *to mysdon hym eftsones* (*if þei mette eftsoone* **B**): *whanne hy next metten* **A** (vii
155).
153   *sowle* (one **B** MS): *soule quaþ peris* **A** (vii 156).
160   *guttus* (**BC**): *mawis* (*wombes* A, *ribbes* V) **A** (vii 163).
162   *botte*: variant form (mainly Western) of *bat*.
163   *that ... swolle: amydde hise lippis* (etc.) **A** (vii 166).
165   "Had not Sir Thirst the physician fetched water sooner...." For the form *furst*
"thirst" see v 106; it could, of course, be the adverb "first," in which case *sire* would be an
(uncancelled) anticipation. No **A** MS has *sire*, but the word order *first the physician* is found
in MAH³. The name "Sir Thirst" is quite appropriate in the context, and it is easy to see
how other **A** MSS would have misunderstood the name as "first." Allegorically, however,
he operates in the opposite way from Hunger, sufficient reason to account for his
elimination in revision.
       yfet watur the sannure: defendite (*fette* WK) *him watir* **A** (vii 168): in **Z**WK the
physician brings water to aid digestion; in **A** he forbids it; in **BC** the line is dropped
entirely.
166   *that they eten: ygrounde* **A** (vii 169).
170   Unique to **Z**: this short line looks like an experiment, intended for expansion.

For a potteful of pesus that Perus had ymaked
An hep of hermytus henten hem spadus,
Ant doluen dryt ant dunge to dutten out Hungur.
175 Blynde ant bedreden were botned a thowsond,
That hadde **be** blynde ant broke-legged be the heye weye.
Hungur hem heled **myt** an ote cake,
Ant lame men lymes were lythed that tyme
Ant becomen knaues to kepe **menne** bestus,
180 Ant preyd por charite wyth Peres for to dwelle,
Al for couetyse of ys corn to cach awey Hungur.
Ant Perus was prowd thereof ant **pulte** hem in offisus,
Ant yaf hem mete ant mone as they myghte disserue.
Thenne haued Perus pite: **a** preyd Hungur to wende
185 Hom into ys oune erd ant halde there euere.
"Ac yut Y prey the," quad Perus, "ar thow passe forthur,
Of beggares ant byddares wat best be to done?
For Y wot wel, be þow went, they wyl wyrche ful ylle:
Meschyf hit makuth they ben so meke nowthe
fol. 137r   Ant for defaute of fode thus faste they wirchen.
191 Ant hit ben my blody brethurne, for God bought us alle:
Trewthe taughte me onus to louey hem vch one,
To helpe hem of alle thing **as they han nede.**
Now wold Y wytte, yf thow wistus, wat were the beste,
195 How Y myghte amaystren hem ant maken hem to wyrche,
Tho that ben staleword ant stronge ant struyores beth holden.
For bedreden ant blynde ant broke-legged wreches
That ben syke ant sory, Y schal yse mysilf

Z 172-195 = A 174-197; Z 196-198.

176 hadde be: (hadde) leiȝe A (vii 178).
    blynde: Kane (p. 448) argues for blereyed.
177 myt: wiþ A (vii 179).
178 men (E): for the gen. pl. without -s, cf. menne 179.
179 menne: peris A (vii 181).
182 pulte: putte A (vii 184); see Appendix, p. 123.
184 a "he": and A (vii 186).
185 erd: supported by Kane (p. 448).
191 alle: at the beginning of 192 in Z.
193 as ... nede: aftir þat hem nediþ (etc.) A (vii 195).
196-201 Unique to Z: cf. Z vii 127-128 and A vii 208-212 (not in Z).

That they haue bred ant brede beddyng ant clot*us*,
200   **Ant kepe hem fro colde, so me Cryst helpe,**
     Ant eke fro hung*ur* ant harme as myn owne chyldre*n*."
     "**Herke** now," q*u*ad Hung*ur*, "ant holde hit for a wysdom.
     Bolde beggares ant bygge that mow here bred byswynke,
     W*y*t*h* hownd*us* bred ant horse bred holde vp here hert*us*;
205   Abaue hem w*y*t*h* benus for bollyng of here wombe,
     Ant yf tho grom*us* gruch, bide hem go ant swynke,
     Ant he schal soupe swett*ur*e wen he yt hath disserued.
| But yf **yt be** eny freke fortune haue apeyred
     W*y*t*h* fuyr or w*y*t*h* fals men, fonde such to knowe.
210   Conforte hym w*y*t*h* thy catel for Crystys loue of heuene;
     Loue hem ant lene hem ant so lawe of kynde wolde."
     "I wolde nat greue God," q*u*ad Perus, "for al the god **that Y welde.**
     Myght Y synneles do as thow seyst?" seyde Perus thenne.
     "Ye, Y byhote God," q*u*ad Hung*ur*, "or elles the bible lyes.
215   Go to Genesis the geaunt, engendrour of vs alle:
     In sudore ant swynk þow schalt thy mete telye
     Ant laborey for thy lyflode, ant so oure lord hyghte.
     Ant Sapience seth the same, Y sey hit in the byble:
     Piger propter frigus no **fode** nolde tylye;
220   A schal go **begged** ant byd ant no man bete ys hung*ur*.
     Mathew w*y*t*h* the mannes face mowtheth these word*us*,
     That *seruus nequam* haued a pnam, ant for a nolde hit vse

Z 199-201; Z 202-211 = A 198-207; [om. A 208-212]; Z 212-222 = A 213-223.

199   *brede*: pt. pp. of *brede* v² "spread."
202   *herke* (*herkne* **C**): *here* **A** (vii 198).
205   *abaue, benus*: supported by Kane (pp. 448-449).
207   *yt*: smudged.
208   *yt be*: *þou fynde* **A** (vii 204).
     freke: *freke þat* **A**.
     haue (subj.): *haþ* **A**.
211   After this line **A** has vii 208-212; cf. **Z** vii 196-201.
212   *that Y welde*: *on ground* **A** (vii 213).
214   *god* (U): *þe* **A** (vii 215).
219   *fode*: *feld, fold, londe, fote, mete* **A** (vii 220); Prov. 20:4 would support any of these, having simply *arare*.
220   *begged*: *begge* (etc.) **A** (vii 221). For the usage, see Mustanoja, pp. 581-582; it is a combination of the types *go walked* + *go abegged* (**C** ix 138).
222   *That*: rejected by Kane (pp. 131, 449), in favour of the less explicit omission of the conjunction.

He haued maugre of ys mayster for eueremore aftur,
Ant bynom hym ys pnam for a nolde wirche,
225   Ant yaf yt hym in haste that hadde ten there byfore,
Ant senes he seyde that ys seruauns hit herde,
'He that hath, schal haue, to helpe there **hym licuth;**
Ant he that nawght hath, schal nawght haue ne no man hym helpe;
Ant he that weneth wel to haue, Y wyl hit hym byreue.'
230   **Of thys matere Y myght make a longe tale,**
Ac h[i]t fallet nat for me, for Y am no dekne
To preche the peple wat that poynt menes.
Kynde Wyt wolde that euery wyght wroughte
Or **to teche or to telle** or trauayle **wyth** handus,
235   Contemplatyf lyf or attyf lyf, Cryst wolde hit alse.
The sawter seyt in salme **in** *beati omnes:*
Labores manuum tuarum quia manducabis.
fol. 137v   **Tow best yblessed of God ant the bet schat thow spede.**
"Yut Y preye the," quad Perus, "por charite, **ant** thow cunne
240   Eny lef of leche craft, lere hit me, **Y bydde.**
| For **Y haue** summe seruauns ben sike otherwyle:
Of al the woke they wyrche nat, so here wombe acuth."
"I wot wel," quad Hungur, "wat sykenesse hem ayleth:
| They han manged ouer muche, that maketh hem to grone,
245   **Ant eke ydronke to depe, that doth hem harme ofte.**

Z 223-229 = **A** 224-230; **Z** 230-232; **Z** 233-237 = **A** 231-234a; [om. **A** 235-236]; **Z** 238;
Z 239-244 = **A** 237-242; **Z** 245.

227   *hym licuth* (**C**): *nede is* (etc.) **A** (vii 228).

230-232   Unique to **Z**.

231   *hit: ht* **Z**. A curl on the *t* of *fallet* may be for an *h. Y am no dekne*: cf. E. T.
Donaldson, *Piers Plowman: the C-Text and its Poet* (New Haven, 1949), pp. 202-203.

233   *euery* (U, one **B** ms): *iche* **A** (vii 231).
    wyght: supported by Kane (p. 449).

234   *teche, telle, trauayle*: **A** has a series of gerunds here, but three mss have the noun
trauaill.
    wyth: of **A** (vii 232).

236   *in* (**B**): *of* **A** (vii 234).

238   Unique to **Z**: replaced in **A** by vii 235-236; both versions refer to Ps. 127.

239   *ant* (**B**): *ʒif* **A** (vii 237).

240   *Y bydde* (*I preye* one **B** ms): *my dere* **A** (vii 238).

241   *Y haue summe seruauns: summe of my seruauntis* **A** (vii 239).

244   *to grone* (*to grone ofte* **B**): *grone ofte* **A** (vii 242).

245   Unique to **Z**.

Ac Y hote the," q*ua*d Hung*ur*, "as thow thyn hele wilnest,
That thow drynke no day ar thow dyne sumwat.
Ette nat, Y hote, ar hung*ur* the **bydde**
Ant sende of ys sauce to sauere w*yth* thy lypp*us*,
250 Ant kep sum **forto** sop*er*tyme ant site nat to longe.
Arys vp ar **thyn** appetyd haue ete ys fulle;
Lat nat sire Sorfet sitte at thy borde:
Lef nat that **liare** for he ys licores of tunge,
Ant af*ur* many manere met*us* ys mawe ys **afyngred.**
255 Ant yf thow diete the thus, Y dar legge myn **eyes**
That fisik schal ys furred hodus for ys fode sille,
Ant eke ys cloke of Calabre w*yth* the cnappus of golde,
Ant be fayn by my fayth ys fysyk to lete,
Ant lerne to labory w*yth* land **for liflode ys swete.**
260 **I defame nat fysyk, for the science ys trewe,**
Ac vncunynge kaytyues that kannen nat rede a lettere
Macuth hem maystres men for to hele.
Ac hit ar maystres morthrares men for to quelle,
Ant none leches but lyares, lord hem amende!
265 **In Ecclesiasticis the clerc that can rede**
May se hit there hymsilf ant senes teche other:
Honora medicum, **he seyt, for** ***necessitatem.***
For helthe from heuene, Y hope, doth out sp*r*inge,
Ant therefor the byble bit ant in ys bok techet

Z 246-259 = **A** 243-256; [om. **A** 257-258]; **Z** 260-269.

248 *bydde: take (hente* N) **A** (vii 245).
250 *forto: til/to/for* **A** (vii 247); see Kane, pp. 445, 446.
251 *thyn:* unique to **Z**, perhaps omitted in **A** so that Appetite would be personified.
253 **W** reads: *Leue not þat lechour for he is likerous of mouþ,* which is close to **Z**. **A** (vii 250) reads: *Loue (Leue) hym nouȝt for he is a lecchour & likerous of tunge* (etc.).
254 *afyngred* "hungry" (many **B** mss): *alongid* **A** (vii 251).
255 *eyes (eie* W): *armes/eres* (**C**)/*hed/lyf* **A** (vii 252).
259 *for liflode ys swete* (all **B** mss): *lest liflode hym faile* **A** (vii 256).
260-278 Unique to **Z**. In place of this lengthy excursus on physicians **A** has two lines (vii 257-258):
Þere arn mo liȝeris þan lechis, lord hem amende.
Þei do men diȝe þoruȝ here drynkes er destenye it wolde (etc.).
264 Cf. **A** vii 257.
267 Ecclus. 38:1.

270   **That leches of lordus scholde here lower haue:**
      A regibus et principibus erit merces eorum –
      Of princes ant prelatus here pencyoun schal aryse,
      Ant of no pore peple no peneworth gode take.
      Ac lewed Lumbardes Londona han aspyed,
275   **That Gloten ys a god there ant greueth men ful ofte,**
      Ant macuht hem maystres ant medecynes schapeth,
      Ant casteth men of the cardyacle into the kyrke yerdus,
      Flemmynges ant Frenche men ant fele of this Englysch."
   ¶   "Be seynt Purnele," quad Perus, "**me payeth wel youre** wordus.
280   Thys ys a louely lesson, lord hit the foryelde!
      Wende now wen thy wille ys, that wyl **the bytyde.**"
      "I behote the," quad Hungur, "that hennes nell Y wende
      Tyl Y haue dyned by thys day ant ydrunke bothe."
      Thenne haued Perus no peny pulletus to bigge,
285   Noythur ges ne grys but to grene chesus,
      A wel, a potteful of wey ant welled croddes,

Z 270-278; **Z** 279-285 = **A** 259-265; **Z** 286 (cf. **A** 266).

270   *lower* "pay": MED *louer* (2).

271   Used again in **Z** VIII 47 (**A** VIII 46a), where it is combined with Ps. 14:5 to refer to lawyers. Its source is not known, but Skeat's closest analogue is Ecclus. 38:2 (cf. on line 267 above) "*A Deo est enim omnis medela, et a rege accipiet donationem,*" referring specifically to doctors. Hugo of St. Cher glosses *in conspectu magnatorum* (Ecclus. 38:3) by the words "*id est, coram principibus et regibus*" (*Opera*, 3 [Venice, 1732], fol. 243v). We owe this reference to Dr. Anne Quick. The use of the same motif in Passus VIII, but referring to lawyers instead of doctors, could have led to its cancellation here.

274   The Lombards notice that Londoners are gluttonous (and therefore prone to sickness) and see their opportunity to sell them medicines (which will turn out even more harmful). This alludes to Lombardy's reputation for manufacturing poisons. See Lynn Thorndike, *A History of Magic and Experimental Science*, 3 (New York, 1934), 526: "Not only, with the waning of Montpellier, did the medical schools of north Italy take the lead, but Lombardy had a bad contemporary [= fourteenth century] reputation for sorcery and poisoning." Thorndike cites the *Chroniques de S. Denis* (a. 1393) XIV 5: "allegantes quod in Lombardia ... intoxicationes et sortilegia vigebant plus quam aliis partibus." We owe this reference to Dr. Faye Getz.

279   *Purnele*: supported by Kane (p. 449).
     me payeth wel youre: *þise arn profitable* **A** (VII 259).

281   *the betyde* (one **B** MS): *be þou euere* (etc.) **A** (VII 261). *wyl* "well" (cf; IV 89). For *that* + subj. see above on VII 19 and Appendix, p. 125.

283   *Tyl* (all **B** MSS): *Er* **A** (VII 263).

284-286   These lines are in direct speech in **A** (VII 264-265 + 266): "*I haue no peny,*" *quaþ piers,* ... etc.

286   Unique to **Z**: "a well, a potful of whey, and boiled curds," the well perhaps indicating sobriety. Replaced in **A** by VII 266: *A fewe cruddis & crem & an hauer cake.*

"A lof of ben*u*s ant brant **to breke among myn hens**,"

fol. 138r   Ant **sethe a swor by ys sowle he ne had** no salt bakou*n*

Ne no kokenay, by Cryst, colopp*u*s to make.

290   "I haue p*er*sile ant poret ant many pla*n*t koules,

Ant eke a kow ant a calf, ant a cart-mare

To draw a feld dunge, wyle the druye last*u*s.

Ant by thys lyflode Y mot liue til lowmasse tyme,

Ant by that Y hope to haue heruest in my crofte:

295   Thenne may Y dyghte thy dyner as me dere licuth."

Alle the pore peple thenne pese coddus fette,

Benus ant bake apples they broughte*n* in here lappe,

| Chibolles ant chireuilles ant chiries **ful** ripe,

| Ant profredon thys p*re*sent to plese myd Hung*ur*.

300   Hung*ur* ett this in haste ant axed aft*ur* more.

Thenne the folk for fere fetten hym monye

Grene poret ant pesus to peyse hym **for eu*er*e**.

By that yt **neyghled** nere heruest that newe corn cam to chepinge,

Thenne was folk fayn ant fedde Hung*ur* **myt** the beste,

305   W*yth* gode ale ant glotonye gerten hym to slepe.

Ant tho nolde Wastor nat wirche but wandren aboute,

Ne no beggare heten bred that benes in come,

But **yt were** koket or clerematyn or of clene wete,

Ne none halpeny ale in **eny** wyse drynke,

Z 287-309 = **A** 267-289.

287   *brant*: presumably an unrecorded form of *bran*, by back-spelling after the loss of *t* after *n* (cf. Appendix, pp. 122-123.

     to ... hens: *ybake for my children* **A** (vii 267). The **Z** version stresses Piers' poverty; **A**'s emphasizes the pathos of the starving children.

288-289   In **A** (vii 268-269) these lines continue as part of Piers' speech: *And I sei3e be me soule I haue no salt bacoun...* etc.

298   *chiries ful ripe*: *ripe chiries manye* **A** (vii 278).

299   *profredon*: *profride peris* **A** (vii 279).

301   *monye*: so spelled in MSS VChL. **Z**'s spelling system allows either "many" or "money," but Hunger would not naturally be appeased by money.

302   *peyse*: supported by Kane (p. 449).

     for euere: *þei þou3te* (etc.) **A** (vii 282).

303   *neyghled*: this form (from OE *nēalǣcan*) is found in Dan Michel's *Ayenbite of Inwit* (1340), p. 105/31, and thereafter only in **C** xx 58.

304   *myt* (N): *wiþ* **A** (vii 284).

308   *yt were*: om. **A** (vii 288).

309   *eny*: *no* **A** (vii 289).

310 But of the best ant the brownest that **in borw ys to** sille*n*.
    Laborerys that han no land bot liue on here handus
    Deyneden **to day** of nyght olde wort*u*s;
    May no peny ale hem **plese** ne no pese of bakou*n*,
    But yt be fresch flesch or fysch fryed **other bake,**

315 Ant that chaut or ple*u*s chaut, for chillyng of ys mawe.
    Ant thow he be fed w*yth* fresch mete ant of the fynest drynke,
    But he be heyliche yhuyred, elles wol he gruche,
    That he was werkman ywrought waryen the tyme,
    Ant thenne corsen the kyng ant al the consayl aft*u*r

320 Such lawes to loke laboreres to chaste.
    Ac wyle Hung*u*r was here mayst*e*r, wolde no*n* **gruch**
    Ne stryue ayeyen ys statut, so sturnelyche a locud.
    Ac war ye wel, werkmen, wynneth wile ye mow,
    For Hung*u*r hyd*u*rward hasteth hym faste.

325 He schal awake w*yth* wat*e*r **werkme*n*** to **gaste:**
    Ar fyf yer be fulfult such **feym** schal aryse;
    Torw flod ant thorw foul wedur fruytes schulle fayle,
    Ant so seyth Sat*u*rne ant sent yow to warne.

Z 310-315 = **A** 290-295; **Z** 316; **Z** 317-328 = **A** 296-307.

310   *in borw ys to* (most **B** mss): *breusteris* **A** (vii 290). **Z** means: "that there is for sale in the town."

311   Kane (p. 449) rejects this line (preserved in this form in TH²M, possibly others, and some **B** mss) in favour of: *Laboureris þat haue no land to lyue on but here handis* (vii 291), which is a stronger metaphor.

312   In **A** (vii 292) the line reads: *Deyneþ nou3t to dyne a day ni3t olde wortis*, with many variants, including the omission of *nou3t*. The **Z** line can be interpreted variously: first, *deyneden* = "disdained" (MED *deinen* v (2)); then (a) take *to-day* as the equivalent of *a-day* (as in **A**), cf. OED *to* prep. II 7: "disdained night-old worts in the day" (this involves the construction *deinen of*, not in MED); or (b) assume that *dyne a* has beel lost after *to*: this would be similar to mss HLA: "disdained to dine by day on night-old worts." (b) is perhaps the simpler.

313   *plese: paye* **A** (vii 293).

314   *other bake* (all **B** mss, **C**): *or irostid* (etc.) MH³AW: om. **A** (vii 294).

316   Unique to **Z**.

317   *gruche* (R): *chide* **A** (vii 296).

321   *gruch: chide* **A** (vii 300).
      ne stryue cancelled at end of line in **Z**.

323   *Ac ... wel: I warne 3ow* **A** (vii 302).

325   *wyth* (W, all **B** mss): *þoru3* **A** (vii 304).
      werkmen: wastours **A**.
      gaste: chaste **A** (cf. **Z** 320).

326   *feym: famyn* (etc.) **A** (vii 305). **Z**'s form is apparently an unrecorded ME borrowing of Fr *faim*.

Passus Octauus

Trewthte herde telle hereof ant to Perus sente
| To taken ys teme ant telyen erthe,
Ant purchased hym a pardoun *a pena et a culpa*
For hym ant for hys ayres for eremore aftur,
5   Ant bad hym halden hym at hom ant heryen ys leyes.
Ant alle that hym hulpe to herye or to sowe
Or eny manere mestere that myght Perus helpe,
Part of that pardoun the pope hath ygraunted.
Kingus and knyghtus that kepen holy kyrke
10   Ant ryghtfulliche in rewmes reuleth the peple
Han pardoun thorw purgatorye to passe ful sone,
| In paradys wyth patriarchus to pleyen thereaftur.
Bischopus **yblessed that** bothe lawes conuthe
Locun on that one lawe, leren men that othur,
15   Ant bereth hem bothe on here bak as here baner scheweth,
| Prechen here parsonus the perelus of synne,
How that schabbed schep schal here wolle saue,
Han pardoun **myt** the apostlus wen they passe hennes
Ant at the day of dome at hey deys sytte.
20   Marchauns in the margyne haued mony yerus,
But no *pena et a culpa* the pope nolde hem graunte;
For they helde nat here halydayus as holy chyrche **wolde,**

fol. 138v

Z vɪɪɪ 1-22 = **A** vɪɪɪ 1-22.

12   *In paradys wyth patriarchus*: reversed in **A** (vɪɪɪ 12).

13   *yblessed that: þat blissen and* **A** (vɪɪɪ 13; cf. **BC**: *Bysshopes yblessed, if þei ben as þei sholde*). **Z** means: "blessed bishops that know both laws."

18   *myt: wiþ* **A** (vɪɪɪ 18).

21   *pena* (A, two **B** ᴍss): *a pena* **A** (vɪɪɪ 21). The omission of *a* may be simply scribal, but the phrase may have been reduced through common usage.

22   *wolde: techiþ* **A** (vɪɪɪ 22).

   | Ant for they swore by here sowle **ac** so most God hem helpe
     Ayeynes clene conscience here catel to selle.
25 Ac under ys secrete sel Trewthe sente hem a lettre,
     That they scholde bygge baldely wat hem beste licud,
   | Ant sillen hit senn*us* ayeyn ant sauen **here** wynnyg*us*,
     Ant maken mesoun-deux theremyt myseyse men to help,
     Wyked wey*us* wyghtlich*e* to amende,
30 Ant beten brug*us* aboute that tobroke were,
     Maryen maydones or maken hem nonn*us*;
     Pore wydew*us* that wylned **be wedded no more,**
     Fynden hem fode for lordus loue of heuene;
     Sette scoleres to scole or to som skyn*us* crafte;
35 Releuen religioun ant renten hem bettre.
     "Y schal sende yow mysilf seynt Miel myn ang*e*l
     That no deuel schal yow dere, deye wan ye schull*e*,
     That he ne schal sende youre soule saf into heuene
     Ant byfor the face of my fad*ur* fourme youre sete.
40 Huserye ant auarice ant hothus Y defende,
     Ant that no gyle go w*yth* yow but the graythe trewthe."
     Thenne were marchauns mery, mony wopen for ioye
     Ant yeuen Wylle for **thys** wrytyng wollen cloth*us*;

Z 23-43 = **A** 23-43.

23 *ac*: *and* **A** (VIII 23).
    most God: *god muste* **A**.
    The phrase *ac ... helpe* seems to be part of the oath of the merchants: "they swore by
their souls and by 'may God help us';" the syntax is awkward because the oath is placed in
oratio obliqua (cf. **Z** v 99). Either *ac* is used very loosely or, more probably, it is simply an
error for *and* or for *al* (MED *also* 1d (a), although according to MED the form in oaths is
always *as*, never *also*; see OED *so* 19 (a), but again no example with *also* is cited).
26 *That they scholde* (all **B** MSS): *And bad hem* **A** (VIII 26).
27 *sillen hit sennus*: *siþen selle it* **A** (VIII 27).
    For the spelling *wynnygus*, cf. III 166 and Appendix, p. 123.
28 *men* (A, C): *folk* most **B** MSS: om. **A** (VIII 28).
30 *beten*: Kane (pp. 160-161, 450) argues for the technical term *bynde*.
32 *be wedded no more*: *not be wyues aftir* **A** (VIII 32).
37 *schulle* (W): *diʒe* **A** (VIII 37).
38 *he* (U): *I* **A** (VIII 38).
41 *graythe*: supported by Kane (pp. 162-163, 450).
43 *thys*: *his* **A** (VIII 43).

For he coped thus here clause, couth hym gret mede.
45 ¶ Men of lawe haued lest for letred they ben alle,
Ant so seyth the sawter ant Sapience bothe:

Super innocentem munera non accipies: a regibus et principibus
erit merces eorum,

"Of prynces ant prelatus **youre** pencyoun schal aryse,
Ac of no pore peple no peneworth **schal ye** take.
50 Ac that speneth ys speche ant spekoth for the pore
That ys innocent ant nedy ant no man apeyreth,
Conforteth hym in that cas, coueyteth nat ys godus,
But for oure lordus loue lawe for hym schewith,
Schal no deul at ys deth day dere hym a myte
55 That he ne worth sicurly saf, ant so the sawter wyttnesseth.
Ac to bygge water ne wynde ne wyt ys the thridde

fol. 139r | Wolde nere holy writ, God wot the sothe.
Thise thre for thralles ben throw among vs alle
To waxen ant to wanyen were that God licuth.
60 His pardoun in purgatorye ful petit ys, Y trowe,
| That **mercedem** for **ys** motyng of mene men resseyueth.
Ye legystres ant lawyares, lye Yc **now,** trow ye?
| **Ye,** sennes ye seth thus **yowsylf,** seweth **ye** the beste."
Alle lybbeynge laborerus that lyueden by here handus,
65 That trewlyche token ant trewlyche wonnen
| Ant lyueden in loue in lawe for here lowe hert,

Z 44-66 = **A** 44-65.

44 *coped*: Kane (p. 450) discusses the variants *copiede/copide/coupide*; although he adopts *copiede*, he suggests that *copide* may contain a pun.
couth: in effect supported by Kane (p. 450), who argues for *couden*.
47 See note to vII 271 above.
48-49 Indirect speech in **A**, with *here* (for *youre*) in 48, and *to* (for *schal ye*) in 49.
57 *Wolde* (*Nolde* V): *Ne wolde* **A** (vIII 56).
61 *mercedem*: *mede* **A** (vIII 60): see line 47 above.
ys "his": om. **A**.
for ys motyng of mene men: *of mene men for motyng* **A**.
62 *lye ... ye* (M, with *out* "anything" for *now*): *ȝe wyten ȝif I leiȝe* (etc.) **A** (vIII 61).
63 *Ye ... yowsylf*: *Siþen ȝe sen it is þus* **A** (vIII 62).
ye²: *to* (or om.) **A**. In **Z** *thus* may be an error (or back-spelling) for *this*; *yowsylf* is reflexive. The meaning of **Z** is similar to **A**: "Yes, since you see thus for yourselves, follow the best."
64 *lyueden* (Crowley's **B**): *lyuen* (etc.) **A** (vIII 63).
66 *lyueden*: *lyuen* (etc.) **A** (vIII 65).

| Hadden the same absolucioun that sent was Per*us*.
Beggaueres ne byddares ne but nat in the bulle
But yt be in the bak half w*yth*outen, by hemsilue,
70   But yf here suggestioun be soth **wen they schal** begge.
For **at** that begget or byt, but yf he nede haue,
He ys fals w*yth* the fend ant defrauduth the nedy,
Ant eke gyleth the gyuer ageynes ys wille.
| **Thus** they leuen nat ne no lawe **kepen;**
75   **Were they haue haly wat*ur* or haly bred, habbeth they no ward,**
Ant eke vnschryue*n* schrew*us* thyl schyrthorsday at eue.
They wedde none womme*n* that they w*yth* dele,
But as wilde best*us* w*yth* wehe worthen vp togyderes
Ant bryngeth forth barnes that bastard*us* ben holde.
80   Or ys bak or ys boon a brekth in ys youthe
Ant goth ant fayteth **thenne** w*yth* here faunt*us* for euer*e*more aft*ur*.
There ar mo mysschape among*us* hem, ho so tacuth hede,
Thenne of alle oth*ur* man*e*re men that on thys molde wandreth.
Tho that leden thus here lyf mowen lothy the tyme
85 | That euere war they men wro3t, wen they schulle hennes fare.
Ac holde men ant hore that helples ben of strengthe,
Ant womme*n* w*yth* childe that wyrche ne mowe,
Blynde men ant bedereden ant broken in here membris,
That tacut this mischef meklyche **han as myche p*a*rdoun**

Z 67-68 = **A** 66-67; **Z** 69; **Z** 70-74 = **A** 68-72; **Z** 75-76; **Z** 77-89 = **A** 73-85.

68   *beggaueres*: the form is not paralleled. *but* = pr. pl. *beth* "are."

69   Unique to **Z**: "Unless they are on the dorso, outside, by themselves."

70   *wen they schal*: *þat shapiþ hem to* (etc.) **A** (vɪɪɪ 68).

71   *at* (or *ac*): probably read *a* "he" (*he* **A**): the form *at* = *that* appears to be used for the relative pronoun or conjunction only.
     nede haue (M): reversed in **A** (vɪɪɪ 69).

74   *Thus they leuen nat*: *þei lyue nou3t in loue* (etc.) **A** (vɪɪɪ 72); in **Z** *leuen* may be an error for *louen* (*e/o* confusion) or could mean "believe" (i.e., they are unbelievers).
     kepen: *holden* **A**.

75-76   Unique to **Z**: "They have no regard as to whether they have holy water or holy bread, and (remain) unshriven wretches until the evening of Holy Thursday," i.e., they neglect baptism, communion and confession.

79   *bastardus*: Kane (p. 450) argues for *bois* "boys" as the *difficilior lectio*.

81   *thenne*: om. **A** (vɪɪɪ 77).

85   *war they* (*þei were* HV, many **B** mss): *he was* (etc.) **A** (vɪɪɪ 81).

89-90   This weak couplet has been rewritten in **A** (vɪɪɪ 85-86):
     Þat takiþ þis meschief mekliche as myselis & oþere
     Han as pleyn pardoun as þe plou3man hymselue.

90   **As Perkyn the plowman ant yut a poynt more:**
| [For] loue of here **lownesse** oure lord hem hath grauntd
Here penaunce ant here purgatorye vpon thys puyr erth*e*.

<Conclusion by Hand *Q*>

"Pers," q*ua*d a prest tho, "þi p*a*rdou*n* most I rede,
For I wil construe eche clause *and* ke*n*nyt the on Englysche."
95   And Pers at his prey3er the p*a*rdou*n* vnfoldede:
Et qui bona egerunt in vitam eternam, qui vero mala in ingnem
eternum.

In to lynis it lay *and* not a letter more,
And was wrety*n* rith thus in wytten'e'sse of Trewthe.
"Peter," q*ua*d the prest tho, "I can no pardou*n* fynde
100 But do wyl and haue wyl *and* God schal haue þi soule,
And do euyl and haue euyl, hope thow no*n* oder
fol. 139v   That after thi deth day to helle schalt thow wende."
And Pers for pure tene pulled yt asunder and seyde
"*Si ambulauero in medio vmbre mortis non timebo mala, quoniam*
tu mecum es.
105 I schal sesin of my sowyng and swynke not so harde,
Ne aboutyn my lyflode so besi be no more.
Off prey3erys and penau*n*s my plow schal ben hereafter,

Z 90 (cf. **A** 86); **Z** 91-92 = **A** 87-88; **Q** 93-95 = **A** 89-91; [om. **A** 92]; **Q** 96 = **A** 95 + 96;
Q 97-98 = **A** 93-94; **Q** 99-107 = **A** 97-106.

91   *For: Ful* **Z**.
lownesse: lou3 herte **A** (VIII 87).

92   *X* ends with this line: there is no sign of an explicit or colophon. *Q* continues
immediately: see Introduction, pp. 27-30. In the following notes, variants in support of *Q*
are given even when there is more than one MS in support (for policy in the **Z** section, see
Introduction, p. 36); this change in practice is to help discover *Q*'s source.

94   *wil* (J, *wol* many **B** MSS): *shal* **A** (VIII 90).

96-98   96 should follow 98, as in **A**, as the sense requires; *Q*'s line-order also differs
from **A** at 111-112 and 127-128, also involving a Latin quotation. In the text which *Q* was
following the Latin may have been in the margin.

96   *egerunt* (K): *egerunt ibunt* **A** (VIII 95), as sense requires.

103 Most **A** MSS (**A** VIII 101) agree with *Q* in having *and seyde* at the end of this line,
rather than at the beginning of the next.

106 *lyflode*: Kane (p. 450) argues for *belyue* (MH[3]) on the grounds that scribes would
have been unlikely to replace the easier *lyflode*; on the other hand, the scribes of MH[3] may
have been attempting to increase the alliteration.

And belouryn þat I below, or my lyflode fayle.
Þe prophete his payn ehte in penaunce and wepyng
110 Be þat the sawter vs seyth, so dede many othir:
Fuerunt michi lacrime mee panes die ac nocte.
That louyth God lely, his liflode is wel mete,
| And but yf Luk lye, he lernyt vs anothir be foulys, þat we ne scholde
| To besy be aboute to make the wombe ioye:
115 *Ne solliciti sitis,* he seyth in his gospel,
And schewyth be exsaunple vsself **for** to wysse.
The foulys in the firmament, who fynt hem in wynter?
Qwan the frost fresyth, fode hem behouyth;
Haue þei no fode to go to, but God fynth hem alle."
120 "Qwat," quad þe prest to Perkyn, "Petyr, **so** me thynkyt,
Thow art lettryth a lytil. Who lernede the on boke?"
"Abstinence the abysse myn a b c me tawthe,
And Concience cam afterward and kennyd me bettyr."
"Were þou a prest," quad he, "thow mytist preche wan þe lykede:
125 *Quoniam literaturam non cognoui þat myth be thi teme."*
"Lewyd lorel," quad he, "lytil lokyst þou the bybil:
Ecce derisores et iurgia cum eis ne crescant.

Q 108-110 = **A** 107-109; **Q** 111 = **A** 110a; **Q** 112 = **A** 110; **Q** 113-126 = **A** 111-124;
Q 127 = **A** 125a.

108 *below*: supported by Kane (p. 450).
    my lyflode fayle (J): other **A** mss vary on word-order and minutiae.
111-112 Reversed in **A**: cf. 96-98 above.
113-114 These lines present one of the major cruces in the **A**-text. Kane adopts the
reading of ms R, as the one most likely to have caused the extensive variants in the other
mss (discussion p. 450);
        And but ʒif luk leiʒe he leriþ vs anoþer,
        By foules, þat are not besy aboute þe bely ioye (viii 111-112)
It is, however, arguable that *Q* preserves Langland's original draft: the hypermetrical 113
and the non-alliterating 114 would have been enough cause for scribes to rewrite the line.
wombe (for *bely*) is found in UVHJW (with extensive alterations to provide alliteration). A
decision about the authenticity of *Q* does not, of course, affect the status of **Z**.
119 *fode* (J): *garner* (etc.) **A** (viii 117).
120 *so: as* **A** (viii 118).
121 *lettryth* pt. pp.: cf. on **Z**'s and *Q*'s language, Introduction, p. 28, Appendix,
pp. 117, 122.
124 *prest* (VHM, three **B** mss): *prest piers* **A** (viii 122).
127-128 Reversed in **A**: cf. 96-98 above.
127 *Ecce* (**A**): Kane (cf. Prov. 22:10 and some **B** mss) conjectures *Eice*, but Langland
probably wrote *Ecce*, which was "corrected" by a few scribes.

On Salaman sawis lityl þou beholdyst."
The prest and Perkyn eythir aposid othir,
130   And thorow here wordis I wok and waytede aboute,
And saw þe sonne euen south syttyn þat tyme,
Meteles and moneles on Maluerne hillys.
Musyng on þis mater a meyle wey I ȝede;
Many tyme þis metelis hath mad me to stodye
135   And for Pers lif plowman, petowsly in herte,

fol. 140r   For þat I say slepyng, if it so be myth.
Ac Catoun construith nay and canonystris bothe
And seyn be hemself *sompnia ne cures.*
Ac for þe bible berith wytt[ne]s, **wan** Danyel þe prophete
140   Demyd the dremys of a kyng onys
That Nabugodonosor nemyn þis clerkys –
Danyel seyde, "Sere kyng, thi sweuene is to mene
That vnkouþe kyngis schul come þi kyngdome to cleyme;
Among lowere lordis thi londis schul be departid."
145   As Danyel demyd in dede fel it after:
Þe kyng lees his lordschepe and lasse men it hadde.
And Iosep met merueylously how þe mone *and* þe sonne

Q 128 = **A** 125; **Q** 129-147 = **A** 126-143.

128   *lityl*: Kane (p. 451) argues in favour of *seldom*, saying that the unmetrical *lityl* may be the result of dittography from line 126.

129   *eythir aposid* (UJAM): reversed in **A** (vɪɪɪ 126).

130   *wordis: wordist* Q.

133   *mater* (U): *mater meteles* J: *metelis* **A** (vɪɪɪ 130).

135   *lif* (UJ): *loue* **A** (vɪɪɪ 132).
   petowsly (UJ): *pensif* **A**. The UJQ reading ("with piety/pity") is certainly the *difficilior lectio.*

138   *And ... hemself* (many MSS, including UJ): om. **A** (vɪɪɪ 134): Kane (p. 451) regards the words as padding and ignores the line in the numbering.

139-140   Line division shared by UJ: various divisions in **A** (vɪɪɪ 135-136).

139   *wyttnes: wyttens* Q.
   wan: how **A** (vɪɪɪ 136).
   þe prophete (UJ): om. **A**.

140   *Demyd* (several MSS, not UJ): *deuinide* **A**: Kane regards the latter as original (p. 121). Q could be read as *deuiyd,* lacking suspension mark (cf. 145 below).
   onys (UJN): om. **A**.

143   *kyngis* (UJ, *kyng* DCh): *kniȝtis (men* M) **A** (vɪɪɪ 139).

145   *demyd: demyd/deuinide* (etc.) **A** (vɪɪɪ 141); cf. 140 above.
   fel it (J): reversed in **A**.

And the eleuene sterris halsede him alle.
"Beau filx," qu*a*d his fader, "for defaut we schulle,
150   I myself and my sonys, seke þe for nede."
It befel as his fader seyde in Pharaoes tyme
Þat Iosep was justise Egipt to kepe –
Al þis makyt me mychil on metels to þinke
Many tymis at mydnyth wan I scholde slepe,
155   On Pers the plowman and qweche a p*a*rdou*n* he hadde
And how þe prest **inpr*o*ued** it al be pure resou*n*;
And demyd þ*a*t dowel indulgense passyd,
Byenalys *and* trionalys and bischopis letteris.
Dowel at þe day of doom ys dyngneleche vnderfongid;
160   He passith al þe p*a*rdou*n* of seynt Pet*er*is schirche.
Now hat þe pope power p*a*rdou*n* to grau*n*t
The peple wyt*h*oute*n* penau*n*ce to passe to ioy.
        | This is a leef of beleue as lett*er*id me*n* techith:
Quodcumque ligaueris super terram etc.
165   And I beleue lely, oure lord forbede ellys,
Þat p*a*rdou*n* and penau*n*ce *and* pr*e*yeris togydere
Mowe saue soulys þ*a*t haue synnyd seuene sethis dedly.
Ac to trostyn on trionalys, trewly me thinkyth,
fol. 140v   Is not so seker for þe soule, sertys, as is dowel.
170   Therefore I rede ȝou lordis þat riche ben on erthe,
Vpon trust on ȝoure treso*u*r trionalis to haue,
Be ȝe neu*er* þe balder to breke þe ten hestis.

Q 148-172 = **A** 144-167.

153   *mychil* (UJ): om. **A** (vɪɪɪ 149).

156   *in proued* (two words in *Q*; *preued* **BC**): *inpugnid* **A** (vɪɪɪ 152). For the sense "refute," see ᴍᴇᴅ *improven*; the modern sense "improve" would radically affect many interpretations of this well-known crux.

159   *vnderfongid*: this weak pt. pp. (not in ᴏᴇᴅ) is also in J.

162   Kane unnecessarily puts a question mark after *ioy*.

163   *beleue* (J): *oure beleue* **A** (vɪɪɪ 159).
     men: *men vs* **A**.

164   *etc.* (**A**): *erit ligatum & in celis* UVJA (**BC**).

165   *oure* (V): om. **A** (vɪɪɪ 160).

166-167   Line division as in UJ: after *saue / salue* **A** (vɪɪɪ 162-163).
     togydere mowe (UJ): *do* **A** (vɪɪɪ 162).

170   *Therefore* (UJN, two **B** ᴍss): *Forþi* **A** (vɪɪɪ 165).
     lordis (UJ): *renkis* **A**.

And namely ȝe maystris, meyris *and* jugis,
That haue þe welthe of þ*i*s werd, for wise me*n* be holden,
175 Forto p*u*rchase p*a*rdou*n and* þe popis bullys,
At þe dredful day of doom wan dede schul arisyn
And comy*n* alle tofore Crist acou*n*tis to ȝelde,
How þu laddist þi lyf and his lawis keptest,
Qwat þou dost day be day þe doom wil reherse.
180 **Of** a pokeful of p*a*rdou*n* ne no pro*u*incialis letteris,
Thow þou be fondyn i*n* fraternite among þe foure ordres
| And haue indulgence dobblefold, but Dowel helpe
I nolde ȝif for ȝoure p*a*rdou*n* o pies hele.
Þerfor I cou*n*sel al cristin to crien God m*er*cy,
185 And Mary his moder be mene betwene,
Þ*a*t God ȝif vs grace or we gon hennys
Swech werkys to werke wil we ben here
And after oure deth day dowel reh*er*se
| At þe doom þet we deden al as he **vs bad *and* tawthe.**
190 **And þat it so mote be to God p*r*eye we all*e*,**
To vs and all*e* cristin God leue it so beffall*e*. Ame*n*

EXPLICIT VITA ET VISIO PETRI PLOWMAN

Q 173-189 = **A** 168-184; **Q** 190-191.

175   *Forto* (UJ): *To* **A** (vɪɪɪ 170).
178   *lawis* (A, all **B** mss, **C**): *lawe* **A** (vɪɪɪ 173).
179   *dost* (JA, one **B** ms): *dedist* **A** (vɪɪɪ 174).
180   *Of*: om. **A** (vɪɪɪ 175). The syntax is uneven in all mss.
182   *Dowel*: *dowel þe / ȝou* **A** (vɪɪɪ 177).
183   *pardoun* (VJN): *patent / patent of þi pardoun* (etc.) **A** (vɪɪɪ 178).
184   *þerfor* (JAN, two **B** mss): *Forþi* **A** (vɪɪɪ 179).
189   J here reads: *þat we wrowtyn wysely as he vs bad & tawte* Amen.
     doom: *day of dome* **A** (vɪɪɪ 184).
     vs ... tawthe (J, *tauhte* **C**): *hiȝte* (etc.) **A**.
191-192   Unique to *Q*: probably the scribe's addition, as rhyme is unparalleled in
Langland.

Appendix

Language

This appendix describes the language of **Z** (excluding the Q-continuation),[1] with reference only to those features that might have a bearing on provenance or date (e.g., linguistic features that were in transition at this period or that are known dialect criteria). Words cited from lines or phrases peculiar to **Z** are marked with an asterisk *, but the orthography and morphology of the whole text is, in fact, uniform: words, lines and passages peculiar to **Z** show no differences from those shared with the **A**-text. That is, there are no signs of patching such as might be found if the scribe were interpolating passages into a deficient exemplar.

A. MORPHOLOGY

1. PRONOUNS

1st sg.: *I* or *y* (*Y*); written *y*ᶜ at III 35, VIII 62; suffixed in *wylly* IV 5, *saydy* V 25, *woldy* VII 194, *nelly* VII 282 (separated in this edition). In a Norfolk phrase *yk* in *so theyk* V 99.

2nd sg.: *thow* (*tow* III 115, etc.); spellings in *yow* for the nominative are expanded *þow*.[2]

3rd sg. masc.: *he*, but very often *a* Pr 121, I 56, etc. Obl. *hym* (but *hemsylfe* I 59).

3rd sg. fem.: *sche* Pr 103, etc.; *he* Pr 101, II 20, etc.; *a* I 17, II 105, etc.; all three forms (*sche*, *he*, *a*) are found together in III 58-60. The form *a* is West-Midland.[3] Genitive and oblique: *here*.

---

[1] See above, p. 28.
[2] See above, pp. 31, 34.
[3] See S. T. R. O. d'Ardenne, *An Edition of þe Liflade ant te Passiun of Seinte Iuliene* (Liège, 1936), pp. 156-157.

2nd pl.: oblique *yow*; occasionally *ou* I 106, *how* Pr 106, etc.; the forms lacking the initial spirant are West-Midland.[4] Genitive *your*, etc. (*yor* I 103).

3rd pl.: *they* (*hey* III 103 probably an error). Oblique *hem* Pr 21 etc.; genitive *here* Pr 31, etc., *ere* VI 89, *theyr* III 21, etc.[5]

Demonstrative: *that*, pl. *tho* Pr 41, etc.; *thys*, pl. *thys* Pr 83, etc., *this* III 25, *thyse* II 64, *thes* VII 36.

2. Nouns

Pl. and gen. in *-ys*, *-es*, *-us*, *-s* (*days* I 44, et.; cf. *hows* VI 64), even in words which commonly have *-(e)n* in Middle English, such as *eyes* IV *144, v 77, etc., *eres* Pr 84. Exceptions: (i) gen. sg. uninflected: *Marie* II 5, II *100, *Pope* II 22, *Pernele* IV 104, *heuenriche* Pr 28, *sowle* VI 7, *Resoun* v 4, *Thomas* VI 33, *fadur* II *97. (Some may be compounds, e.g., *sowle-hele*.) (ii) gen. pl. uninflected: *men* VII 178, *menne* VII 179 (cf. *mennes* VI 49). (iii) gen. pl. in *-en*: *Iuen* I 10 (misunderstood by scribe), *kynggen* I 51, *wyuen* v 56. (iv) pl. in *-ren*: *chyldren* v 61, VII 201, *childurne* (gen. pl.) IV 105, *brethurne* VII 191.

3. Adjectives and Adverbs

Adjectives in *-ly* and *-y* sometimes form the superlative in *-(l)okest*: *louelokest* I 58, *bourlyokest* III *159, *worthyokest* v *36. This is perhaps a West-Midland feature, arising from the Old English by-form *-lucor, -lucost*.[6]

The scribe once indicates a distinction between *al* adv. and *alle* adj.: see II 96.

4. Verbs

(a) *Prefixes*

(1) *y-* is preserved in the present tense of a few verbs: *yse* IV 75, VI 92, VII 198, *ythryueth* Pr 33, *yknoweth* VI 26.

---

[4] D'Ardenne, *Þe Liflade*, pp. 96, 187.

[5] The possibility that the 3rd person plural nominative is sometimes *a* (cf. d'Ardenne, *Þe Liflade*, p. 98) rests on II 8, where *a standʒ* may mean "he stands" or "they stand"; at I 29 the abbreviation *-ʒ* is for *-e* in pt. pp. *yholde*, which would support the idea that in II 8 *standʒ* is plural *stande*. On the other hand, Holy Church may be referring only to Falsehood, and *-ʒ* may be for *-et*.

[6] See Norman Davis (ed.), *Sir Gawain and the Green Knight* (Oxford, 1967), p. 144.

(2) *y-* is often found in the pt. pp., even in words of French origin, e.g., *yrobed* II 17, *yporfyled* II 13, *yrehersed* IV 149.

(b) *Suffixes*

Pr 2 sg.: *-(e)st, -yst; -es* in *wylnes* II *10 (cf. *wystus* [abbreviated] VII 194).

Pr 3 sg.: (1) *-(e)th, -yth,* with variants in *-t, -ht, -d* (see on Consonants), e.g., *hasket* Pr 20, *dryueht* Pr 92, *haued* I 43, *hatted* VI 82, *wytnesset* I 82. (2) Syncopated and contracted, e.g., *byt* I 87, *ryt* IV 14, *last* III *124, *fynt* IV 116, *brekth* IV 45, *berth* IV 45, *sent* VII 328. (3) *-es: menes* Pr *94, *standes* Pr *99, Pr 137, etc. (4) *standʒ* II 8 probably = *standet*.[7]

Pr. pl.: (1) *-eth, -yth,* with variants as for pr. 3 sg., e.g., *conneht* Pr 34, *sekut* V 69, etc. (2) *-es: rennes* II 153, *libbes* II 157, *reykes* IV *158. (3) *-(e)n: dystruyen* Pr 23, *seen* Pr 138, etc. (4) *-e, -( ): lyue, lere* Pr 56, etc.

Imper. pl.: *-eth,* with variants as for pr. 3 sg.: *wythet, wytnesseth* II 65, *sekut* V 71, *spynneth, sparet* VII 11, etc.

Pr. pp.: *-yng* normally; *-end* in *cryend* V 153.

Pt. pp.: (1) weak: *-ed, -yd* (-*ud* sometimes in Weak 2, below), with variants in *-t, -th* (see on Consonants), e.g., *handlet* II 107, *wageth* IV 89, etc. (2) Strong: *-e, -(e)n: ybete* IV 82, *yholde* IV 106, *faren* VII 92, etc.

Infin.: *-e, -en: here* IV 108, *drawen* IV 110, etc.

(c) *Conjugations*

(1) Weak verbs of Class 2: Weak Class 2 verbs with short root vowels usually retain the *i*-element in the appropriate position: e.g., *louy* I 80, *louyen* IV 103 (cf. *louey* VII 192, *loueyen* VI 38), *wonyes* I 6, *wonyen* II 78, pl. *wonyeth* III 12 (3rd sg. *woneth* II 213), *tholye* IV 73, *gladyen* VII 106, *erye* VII 103, *heryen* VII 93 (but infin. *ere* VII 4), pl. *eryeth* VII 122. The *i*-element has been lost from Weak Class 2 verbs with long root vowel: infin. *loke* II 108, 129. The pt. of Weak Class 2 verbs is usually in *-ed-,* but *-ud-* in *pleyuden* Pr 21, *preyude* V *92, *locud* V 79. In the pt. the verb MAKE has both contracted and uncontracted forms: *ymaked* Pr 15, II 63, *ymad* II 30, *mad* II 26, *made* IV 92.

(2) Verbs with geminate consonants (including original Class 3 weak verbs and strong verbs with weak present systems). The original geminate consonants are often retained:

HAVE: infin. *haue* Pr 63, pr. 1 sg. *haue* I 131, pr. 2 sg. *ast* III *156, pr. 3 sg. *hath* II 20, *haueth* I 20, pr. pl. *habbeth* I 107, *an* Pr *99, pt. *haued* I 14, *haueden* Pr 52, etc.

---

[7] See note 5 above.

LIVE: infin. *libbe* v 18, pr. 1 sg. *lyue* v 18, pr. pl. *lybbyth* Pr *83, *leueth* Pr 36, pt. *leueden* Pr 27, pr. pp. *libbynge* Pr 90.

SAY usually *sey, say,* but note: infin. *segge* II 61, IV 123, v 2, pr. 1 sg. *seg* IV 59, pr. 3 sg. *seth* VII 218.

LIE (OE *licgan*): infin. or subj. pl. *lygge* II 108, pr. 3 sg. *lyges* III 111, *ligeth* VII 14, ? subj. pr. pl. *lye* II 29.

BUY: the original geminate consonant of OE *bycgan* is always retained: *byggen* III *160, etc. (for further examples, see on OE *y* below).

(3) Strong verbs: the distinctions between pt. sg. and pt. pl., and between pt. 2 sg. and pt. 1/3 sg. are often retained; some verbs which later "went weak" are still strong.

Class 1: pt. pp. *ygrype* III 117.

Class 2: pt. pl. *chosen* Pr 33.

Class 3: pt. 1 sg. *fond* Pr 18, pt. pl. *songen* VII 102, pt. pl. *swonken* Pr 22, pt. pl. *ronne* Pr *57 (present forms are in *ren-*), pt. 2 sg. *corue* III *153, pt. pl. *holpen* VII 93, 103, *hulpe* VIII 6, pt. 3 sg. *tobarst* v *39, pt. pl. *foughten* Pr 39, pt. 1 sg. *wonne* VII *87, pt. pl. *wonnen* Pr 23, pt. pl. *swolle* VII *163.

Class 4: pt. 2 sg. *bere* III 134, pt. 3 sg. *bar* II 6, pt. pl. *beren* Pr *53, pt. 1 sg. *noem* v *98, pt. pl. *nomen* IV 65, pt. 3 sg. *cam* VII 303, subj. pt. pl. *come* VII 307, subj. pt. *ouerecome* v *94.

Class 5: pt. pl. *beden* III 27, pt. pp. *bede* II 38, pt. pl. *speke* II 206, pt. pl. *setten* VII 102, infin. *gyue* II 91, subj. pr. 3 sg. *yf* III 101, pr. pl. *gyuen* Pr 82, pt. 2 sg. *gef* III 117, pt. 3 sg. *yaf* Pr 106, *gaf* II 167, II 203, pt. pp. *gyue* II 92, *ygyue* II 122, *yf* v 108, pr. 3 sg. *foryth* "forgets" I 123 (see note), (SEE) pt. 1 sg. *sey* Pr 5, *say* Pr 60, pt. 3 sg. *sey* II 159. (On LIE, see above on verbs with geminate consonants.)

Class 6: pt. 1 sg. *schope* Pr 2, pt. pl. *woschen* II 201.

Class 7: pt. 3 sg. *wep* v 132, *weped* IV 62, pt. pl. *wopen* VIII 42, pt. 3 sg. *bete* VII 160, pt. 3 sg. *lep* II 196 (infin. *lepe* v 149), pt. 3 sg. *befel* Pr 7, *fulle* I 60, *byful* v 145, infin. *fong* VI 33, pt. pl. *hongen* I 97, pt. pp. *ysowen* VI 19, pr. 3 sg. *hette* VII 44, *hatted* VI 82, pt. 3 sg. *highte* VII 62, pt. pp. *hote* I 6, *yhote* III *10, pt. pp. *slepe* v 22.

(4) Preterite-present and irregular verbs:

MAY: pr. 2 sg. *myght* II 31, VII 31, *myghtest* Pr 68, pr. pl. *mow* I 70.

MOTE: pr. 2 pl. *mot* I 76.

SHALL: pr. 2 sg. *schalt* VI 45, *schat* VI 48, VII *238, pr. pl. *schul* II 149, *schulle* II 146, VII 327, *schal* Pr 60, II 125, III 152.

CAN: pr. 2 sg. *canst* II 33, pr. pl. *konnen* I 119, *kannen* VII *261.

WILL: pr. 2 sg. *wylt* II 31, *wolte* III 47, *wyl* III 115, *wolle* (*wolle þow nelle þow*) VII 140, pr. pl. *wyl* III 17.

BE: pr. pl. *ben* I 113, II 31, *beth* I 119, *but* VIII 68, *aren* Pr 112, I 113, *ar* I 30.

YEDE (pt.): pt. pl. *yede* Pr 37, subj. pt. 3 sg. *yede* I 16.

B. PHONOLOGY

As with the Morphology, this description is selective and deals only with features that are significant for date and/or dialect or that are idiosyncratic in some way. Apparent *e/o* confusion and extra *i*'s may be purely scribal slips.

1. VOWELS

(1) Late OE /ā/ (from OE *ā* or *a* lengthened before a consonant group) normally appears as *o* (e.g., *tolde* II 161), but as *a* in *halden* I 48, VIII 5, *halde* V 122, *haldeth* II 43 (beside *hold* II 112), *baldely* VII *61, *haly* VIII *75 (twice, perhaps shortened, beside normal *holy*); shortened to /a/ in *hammard* III 132, *nawher* Pr *17. Note also *ar* "before" II 89, V 120 (comp. *arre* IV *4), beside *or* I 69: at V 79 *or* seems to have been altered to *ar*. *er* I 72 is from *ǣr*.

(2) *ǣ¹* and *ǣ²* normally appear as *e* (rarely *ee*): pt. pl. *beren* Pr *53, *speke* II 206, *techeth* Pr 104, *falsede* II *3, *falseed* I 7, etc. *ǣ²* is shortened to *a*: *lasse* II 32, III 140 (but *faytles* II 102), *agast* II 192, pt. *ladde* III *10, *last* "lest" V 67, VII 133, *wrathen* II 88, *lady* III *54, 101, etc. (but *ledy* V 87, *laydy* Pr 95). *ǣ¹* is presumably short in *dredful* I 2; OE *rǣdan* (originally with *ǣ¹*) may have been influenced by *lǣdan*: pt. sg. *radde* V 66, ? pt. subj. *radde* IV 5, pt. pl. *raden* IV 99. The word LET (which had *ǣ¹* in OE) appears as follows: infin. *lete* V *95, *leten* V 126, pr. 3 sg. *lateth* I 125, pt. *lat* II 144, imper. *lat* II 150.

(3) a° before nasals (both alone and in lengthening groups) appears both as *a* and *o*: *monye* Pr 26, *manye* Pr 86, *thonkyng* II 122, *fram* II 124, *lankart* II 152, *londus* II *42, *handus* VII *67, *stande* Pr *71, VII 99, etc. Variation between *a* and *au* is seen in words of French origin: *laumpe* I 116, *pennaunses* Pr 26, *retenanse* II 37, etc. The *i*-mutation of *a* before nasal is *e*: *lengur* I 132, *peny* VII *282, 313 (but *pans* II 203, III 98).

(4) There is only one unambiguous case of lowering of *er*: *sarmon* V *75 (cf. *bern* VII 61, etc.).

(5) ME /ō̧/ and /ō̦/ (from OE *ā*) normally appear as *o*, but as *oe* in: *foet* VII 2, *noem* "took" V *98, *noen* "noon" VII 132, 134, *loef* "loaf" VII *107

(beside *lof* VII 161), *noen* "none" I 113, II *40, etc. (*neen* Pr *54 is from OE *nǣnig*), *lyfloede* I *127 (beside *lyflode* VII 259).

(6) OE *ȳ* (from the *i*-mutation of *u*) appears usually as *y* or *i*, e.g., *hilles* Pr 68, but sometimes as *e* or *u*: *besy* Pr 98, *fulfelle* VII 38 (*fulfult* VII 326), *abegge* VII *66 (*abigge* VII 148, *byggen* III *160, *bugge* III *32), *furste* II 79, *gult* III 8, 44, *murthe* III 11, *murthus* Pr 34, *murgust* II 104, *murye* I 87, *byschutten* II 194, *muche* IV 151, *muchyl* V 141 (*myche* Pr 123, II *3), *vchone* "each one" Pr 108; for WORK see below on *w-r*.

(7) ME /ü/ (from OE *ȳ*, OF *ui*, *ü*) appears usually as *ui*, *uy*,[8] occasionally as *eu* (*ew*): *fuyr* VI *72, *luyther* V 105, *pruide* Pr 24, *pruyde* II 67, *huyre* II 94, VI 25, *buyrde* "woman" III 14, *dystruyen* Pr 23, *nuyest* II 99, *nuyed* II 20, *duyreth* VII 51 (*deure* II *72), *druyeth* "is dry" Pr 116, *puyre* "pure" IV 84, *comewn* III 68; as *u* in *yut* "yet" I 92, etc., *akusseth* "accuses" III 109; on *buyrnes* see below; *wuiman* II 12 is probably a slip.

(8) Early ME /ö/ (OE *ēo*, OF *ö*) is usually *e*, e.g., *byheld* Pr 14, but sometimes *u*: *fulle* "fell" I 60, *byful* V 145 (*befel* Pr 7), *puple* Pr 44 (*peple* I 94), pr. pl. *but* "are" VIII 68. Also note *deul* "sorrow" VII 109. The spelling *buyrnes* V *38 (OE *beorn*) seems to show eo > ēo > u > ü.

(9) Shortening/lengthening and raising/lowering produce alternation between *e* and *i*: (a) /ē̜/ sometimes appears as *i* or *y*: *syknesse* V 119, *mikelyche* I 93, *by* "be" II 57, *scheryue* II 137; (b) /ĕ/ appears as *y*: *hynde* "end" III 97, *wyl* "well" IV 89, VII 119, *bygares* "beggars" II 53; (c) /ī/ appears as *e*: *yleke* "like" I 36, *lecuth* Pr 130 (*liken* Pr 78), *scheryue* II 137; (d) /ĭ/ appears as *e*: *deden* Pr *54, *leueth* "lives" Pr *36, *leueden* Pr 27 (for other forms see above on LIVE), *weten* II *2 (*wytte* II *10, 31), *telyen* VIII 2, *telye* VII 216 (*tylye* VII 219), *wyrschepe* Pr 107.

(10) ME diphthongs in /ei/ which are subject to raising to /ī/ are usually spelled *ey*: *deye* I 90, *heye* I 97, *hey* Pr *99, *sey* "saw" Pr 5 (*say* Pr 60), but LIE ("tell lies") always has *y*: *lye* Pr 52, *lyare* Pr 126, II 153, etc. The converse, *weye* VI 9, etc. (OE *wiga*) is explained by Jordan as Northern,[9] but may be a back-spelling. *noythur* Pr *35 (*nayther* IV 115) may result from *e*/*o* confusion.

(11) ME diphthongs in /au/, /ou/, appear regularly as *au*, *aw*, *ou*, *ow*. In *wroght* I 27 (beside *wrowghte* I 92, *wrowt* III 42) the *oght* graph is probably indication of the diphthong (see below on /ht/).

---

[8] R. Jordan, *Handbook of Middle English Grammar: Phonology*, translated and revised by E. J. Crook (The Hague, 1974), p. 69 ♯ 42 Anm. 1, notes that *ui*, *uy*, for *ȳ* are characteristic of the Vernon MS and MS Laud misc. 108.

[9] Jordan, *Handbook*, p. 122 ♯ 100.

(12) OE *sel-* appears as *y* or *i*, never *u*: *selle* III *149 (*sylle* III 134, *sillen* VIII 27, *syllares* II 53), *selue* III *153 (*sylf* Pr 76, *syluen* I 58). OE *secgan* produces only *e* (see above on SAY).

(13) Influence of *w*: in the *w-r* group there is considerable variation: *swerd* I 45, *wercus* Pr 3, *wers* VI 34, *werld* Pr 127 (*world* Pr 4, 20), *werd* (? "word, world") V *43, *wyrschepe* Pr 107. The word WORK appears variously: *wyrche* I *23, *wyrcheth* I 66, *wurcheth* II 106, *werchyn* I 27. Rounding and loss of *w* is seen in *such* I 15 (beside *seche* Pr 33).

(14) *e* appears for expected *u* in: *jeroures* "jurors" Pr *70, *vnpensched* "unpunished" IV 138, *anhendret* "a hundred" V 162.

(15) Variation between *e* and *a* is seen in: *wannes* VI 1, *wan* I 30, *wen* Pr 117, I 130, *thenne* "then" II *62, *then* "than" I 110.

(16) Various vowel losses or alterations occur in weak stress: suffixal *-ar(e)* in *myllares* Pr *89, *webbestares* Pr 87, *weuares* Pr 87, and most odd *beggaueres* VIII 68 (beside *baksteres*, *bocheres*, *brewstres* Pr 86, etc.); *throute* "thereout" VI 61, *heune* "heaven" I 128, II 5, *deul* "devil" II 84, VIII 54, *polsche* V 148, *ypolsched* VI *80, *benfetus* VI 97, *an* "on" Pr 14, etc. (*a* Pr 35), *sen* "since" Pr 62 (*senes* VII 57). The monophthong *sent* "saint" II *80 (cf. *senne* I 29 note) probably arose in weak stress.

(17) The following unusual forms occur: *commiers* II 52, *kyingus* II 161, *wuiman* II 12, *kyindely* I 26 (all perhaps simply showing an otiose minim); *sannure* "sooner" VII *165 (in OED); *feuld* "field" II 48, *lowmasse* "Lammas" VII 293, *lowedenesse* III 34 (perhaps *e/o* confusion), *lound* "land" VI *78 (perhaps via French: cf. *lawnde* II *47), *warryoke* IV 20, *Jemes* Pr 50 (*James* IV 111 etc.), *Miel* "Michael" VIII 36.

2. CONSONANTS

One of the most striking features of the spelling consists in aspects of the letter *h* – its unetymological presence or absence initially,[10] confusion between *t* and *th*, varied spellings for /ht/ and *d/th* confusion. These four phenomena are dealt with first.

(a) *Aspects of the Letter H*

(1) Initial *h*: *an* "have" Pr *99, pr. 2 sg. *ast* III *156 (*hast* II 92), *ys* "his" IV 33, *his* "is" Pr 127, I 2, *hasket* "asks" Pr 20, *hasketh* Pr *58, *hasked* Pr 136, *houre* "our" Pr 27, *hor* "before" I 16, *how* "you" Pr 106, etc.

---

[10] The scribe went back over the text and frequently inserted initial *h* (often unetymologically); see above, p. 31.

(2) *t/th* variation: *to* "when" IV 149, *torw* "through" I 59, *thecheth* Pr 126, I 28 (*techeth* Pr 104), *tho* "to" VI 95, *guth* "gut" Pr 124, *lifth* "left" II 8, *wyt* "with" II 120, etc.

(3) Spellings for /ht/, etc.: the /h/ element has been lost in *dowtres* Pr 119, *knytes* V 19, but has left its mark (in various forms) in most spellings: *wrowghte* I 92, *lawʒte* III 25, *sygth* I 2, *plyhten* Pr 49, *mygthe* I 53, *hygte* Pr 108, *ysougwth* VI *3. Consequently, for /th/, we see: *mouht* Pr 69, pr. pl. *conneht* Pr 34, *lythth* "tells lies" III 93, *rewʒthe* "pity" IV 102, *hatht* "has" II 14, and similar confusions.

(4) *th/d* variation: in the -*dr*-/-*thr*- groups *d* predominates: *fader* Pr 105, *modur* V 153, *hydurward* VII 324, *thydur* V 155, *wedur* VII 32, but *morthre* IV 43, *morthrares* VII *263; in final position, *staleword* VII *196. There is some confusion between the suffixes -*ed* and -*eth*: e.g., pt. pp. *wageth* IV 89, pr. pl. *fouled* VII 133, pr. 3 sg. *hatted* VI 82.

(5) /th/ > /f/ is seen in *furst* "thirst" V 106; see also VII 165, note.

(6) /hw/ invariably appears as *w*: *wat* I 14, *wen* Pr 1, 117, *were* Pr 13, *wam* Pr 132, *wyche* (OE *hwicce*) IV 104, etc. See also V 124 note.

(7) /w/ has been lost in *ho* I 4, 33, etc. (*wo* VII 1), *to* "two" Pr *64, *such* I 15.

(b) *Palatal Spirants (Voiced and Voiceless), Fricatives and Sibilants*

(8) OE *ġ* appears normally as *y*: *yaf* Pr 106, *yatus* V *39, *aye* IV 32, *ayeyne* IV 36, etc.; it is lost before /i/ in *yf* "give" III 101, pt. pp. *yf* "given" V 108, *yftus* "gifts" I 49, II 123, *foryth* "forgets" I 123 (see note). Forms in *g* are also found, both where required by alliteration (*gyuen* Pr 82, *gyue* II 91-92, *gaf* II 167) and elsewhere (*gaf* II 203).

(9) The voiceless velar/palatal spirant appears variously: *thowʒ* "though" V 126, *thow* Pr 101, *thouʒ* I 103, *they* (OE *þēah*) III 103, *lawen* "laugh" IV 95 (*lawʒe* IV *18, *lawghed* IV 153). See above, Vowels (11), Consonants (3).

(10) The palatal fricative is normally *ch* (*wyrche*, etc.), but *schast* "chaste" I 104. For alliteration *k* is found in *kyrke* V 19, VII 29, 78, *277.[11]

(11) The palatal sibilant is normally *sch*, but note also *wurcheped* III 12, *lordchepe* II 68, *scollen* I 66, *felawscipe* I 60, *screwe* IV 99.

(c) *Loss of Consonants, Simplification, Unvoicing, etc.*

(12) Post-vocalic *n* is often lost, especially in final position: *heue* I 61, *eleue* II 209 (*elleuene* III 116), *sweue* Pr 12, *adow* V 25, *sethe* II *118, *swowe* V 110, *bow* II 133 (*boun* II *60), *ywowden* V 160 (*wownden* II 201),

[11] See Kane, A-text, p. 157.

toknyg v 46, *wynnygge* III 166, *wynnygus* VIII 27; in unstressed words: *me* "one" III 66, *y* "in" III *149, *a* "on" IV 145, etc.

(13) Loss and assimilation of other consonants is sporadic: *seyn* v 69 (*seynt* I 36, etc.), *senne* I 29 (see note), conversely *brant* "bran" VII *287, *nere* "never" Pr 13, etc., *were* "whether" Pr 135, etc., *hammard* "homeward" III 132, *mylelyche* I 91, *stowlyche* III 158, *hensong* "evensong" v 123, *sen* Pr 62, *hed* Pr 80 (*heued* II 181), *hef* "after" IV 96, *attyf* "active" VII 235, *machaunt* IV 117 (*marchawns* II 193), *an* "and" I 41, II 51. Note unsyncopated *monek* v 121. *a* "of" II 25. For retention of geminates, see above on Verbs.

(14) Final unvoicing is seen in *thynk* I 85 (in combination, *lankart* II 152), *lef* "believe" Pr 126, *ant* "and" (usual form), *sent* II 204, *wenten* IV 64, and is implied by the back-spelling *hard* "art" I 29 (see note).

(15) Metathesis: *yhapsed* I 120, *dryt* VII 174, *forst* VI *74.

(16) Epenthetic vowels: *ereth* Pr 108, *berew* VI 54 (*borw* IV 78, *thorw* II 127, etc.).

(17) Other: *asyngne* IV 111 (*sygne* IV 114), *delyt* III *163 (*delys* III *161).

C. VOCABULARY

As this section concerns words, phrases and lines peculiar to **Z**, the asterisk is not used. The lexicon peculiar to **Z** is consistent with Langland's usage in the **A**, **B** and **C** texts; many words and phrases are found elsewhere in Langland, but not in a quantity that would suggest a scribal pastiche. There are *hapax legomena*, archaic words, particularly Langlandian and poetic words, terms from daily life, "modern" words – in short, the kind of lexicon that would emerge from a study of Langland as a whole.

1. Hapax Legomena

feym "hunger" VII 326, *faytles* "without deeds" II 103 (from ME *fet*), *stuty* "hesitant" IV 125 (apparently connected with West-Midland *stutten*), *bewsoun* ? "fine fellows" III 158, *wit* "drive away" VII 59 (unknown origin), *ourf-fors* "ox-tracks" VII 64.

2. Archaic Words

totraye "torment" v 113 (one citation in OED, a1250). Many **Z** words (some found elsewhere in Langland) do not survive long after this period: *tyleth* "extend" VII 66, *steme* "stop" VI 75 (OED v²), *pulte* "push" VII 182 (**B**-text, Laud MS, VIII 98), *neyghled* "approached" VII 303 (**C** xx 58), *ofsent* "send for" II 39 (in some **A** MSS here; last OED quotation c1380; cf. III 38). **Z** uses *ac* and *myd* frequently; MED records only two examples of *ac* after 1400, and notes that *mid* is rare after 1400.

3. LANGLANDIAN AND POETIC WORDS

Poetic words for "man" (*weye, buyrne, freke, gome*) are all found in **Z**; *bakken* "clothe oneself" III 160 is recorded in this sense only in **A** XI 188. The phrase *harneys to pyke* VII 67 is seen in the noun *pykeharneys* **B** XX 263. *lower* "hire" VII 270 occurs only in poetry.

4. TERMS FROM DAILY LIFE

Langland frequently uses terms from everyday life; in **Z** we find *bornet, blanket* III 159, *cammokes* "rest-harrow" (the plant) VII 91 (also in **B** XIX 312, **C** XXII 314), *meble* II 56, *lesewe* II 47, *eggen* VII 58.

5. "MODERN" WORDS

The following antedate OED and MED citations, though the words themselves are doubtless older: *morgage* v. III 96, v 101, *nysotes* "fools" II 99, *clumse* adj. VII 54 (verb used in **B** XIV 52), *sowsest* "steep (in sin)" II 100 (first found in Trevisa; transferred uses not recorded by OED till seventeenth century).

6. OTHER

The form *botte* "bat" VII 162 seems exclusively Western, according to MED citations; the form *dome* v. I 31 is recorded by MED: in **Z** it could be another example of *e/o* confusion. At **Z** III 36 *cleketh* may be "cluck" (as of a hen: OED *clack* v.[1]): this interpretation would suit many MSS of **A** and **B**.

D. STYLE AND SYNTAX

No comprehensive description of the syntax of *Piers Plowman* has yet been published; a comparative account of **Z**'s syntax would therefore be pointless. Furthermore, the minute linguistic features that make up "syntax" and "style" are particularly liable to scribal interference: to describe **Z**'s syntax may, in fact, simply be to describe that of the scribe. A few words may be helpful, however, to show that the syntax of **Z** resembles that of the other versions of the poem. Langland's style is generally recognized to be (in contrast with more "grammatical" authors) notably asyndetic, elliptic, and anacoluthic; **Z** exhibits all these features, many of which are used by Kane and Kane-Donaldson to establish genuine readings according to a criterion by which the "less explicit" syntax is preferred. The following analysis uses passages peculiar to **Z** and passages in which **Z** differs slightly from the agreed reading of **A**. For comparison, examples are sometimes given from lines shared with **A**: these are indicated by (**A**).

(1) Asyndeton (non-expression of connectives) in contrast with **A**: Pr 22, 78, ɪ 90, ɪɪ 193, 200, 201, 213, etc. Conversely **Z** sometimes has connectives not found in **A**: ɪɪ 57 (*Ant*), ɪɪ 106, 208 (*Ac*), etc.

(2) Non-expression of conjunctions, in contrast with **A**: ɪ 109 (*For*), ɪɪ 147 (*For*, but cf. 146), v 89 (*wyth: wiþ þat* **A**); the conjunction *that* is omitted (as often in **A**) at ɪv *152, vɪɪ 288; conversely, note *That* vɪɪ 222 (rejected by Kane), *wat that* ɪ 17 (*what* **A**). **Z** commonly uses *ant* "if": ɪɪ 185 (*and ʒif* **A**), vɪɪ 239 (*ʒif* **A**).

(3) Non-expression of preposition: Pr 125 *leue ... the soule* "dear to the soul" (*lef ... to þe soule* **A**), ɪɪ 202 *Sonendayus* (*on sundais* **A**), v 87 *oure ledy cryed* (*to/on oure lady criede* **A**). Omission in a relative clause: v 86 (**A**).

(4) Non-expression of articles, in contrast with **A**: Pr 19 (adjectives in **Z**), Pr 74 (*prest: a prest* **A**), ɪ 46 (*profession: þe professioun* **A**), ɪ 125 (*lok: þe lok* **A**), ɪɪ 171 and ɪɪɪ 17 (as though *kyng* were a name), ɪɪɪ 93 (*lawe: þe lawe* **A**).

(5) Non-expression of finite verb: ɪ 13 (sc. *is* or *ar*, or emend), ɪ *65 (sc. *is*), vɪɪɪ *76 (sc. *are*); see also note to vɪɪ 127. Non-expression of infinitive after auxiliary verb: vɪ *71 after *wolde*; cf. vɪ 85 after *schal* (**A**).

(6) Non-expression of pronouns: (i) subject pronoun, where noun or pronoun is easily understood: Pr 32, *73, ɪ 7, 122-123, ɪɪ 190, ɪɪɪ 76, etc.; object pronoun, similarly, ɪv 41. (ii) 2nd person sg., where verbal inflexion indicates pronoun: Pr 97, ɪ 21, ɪɪɪ 43. (iii) with change of subject: Pr 120 with change of case (**A**), ɪɪ 124 (**A**), ɪɪɪ *156, v *40, v 83 (**A**). (iv) relative pronoun, subject: v 113 (**A**), vɪ 92 (**A**), vɪ *41, 55, vɪɪ 241; relative pronoun, object: vɪ 84 (**A**), vɪɪ 208.

(7) Other ellipses: ɪɪɪ 53 verb of asking understood (**A**), ɪɪɪ 95 exclamation (**A**), ɪɪɪ *96 where verb acts as noun, v 127 where *than* = "before" (sc. *ar*), vɪ 56 (unless it is corrupt), where positive verb contains an implied prohibition, vɪ *77 where a negative is omitted before a series of negatives. Cf. Pr 67 and note (perhaps a case of aposiopesis).

(8) Imperative formed by *that* + subjunctive: vɪɪ *19 (see note), vɪɪ 281 (cf. **A**), cf. ɪv 7 (**A**). In the following cases *that* + subjunctive (or modal auxiliary) is followed by *to* + infinitive: ɪɪ 59-*60, ɪv 112-114, v *99-100; cf. v 17-18.

(9) Other points of syntax are mentioned in the notes: VII 54 (*for* + adjective), VII 81 (*holdyng* used in a passive sense), VII 113 (*ygraced be*), VII 220 (*go begged*), VIII 23 (oath treated as a substantive). Some awkward passages may be explained as the result of ellipsis: v 46, v 27; at VI 35 *Ac* may mean "if" (or be an error for *ant*), but may mean: "but you want to go – I will guide you."

E. CONCLUSIONS

The whole text of **Z** presents a uniform linguistic appearance, in morphology, phonology, vocabulary and syntax; the passages peculiar to **Z** show no signs of being alien to the remainder. The uniformity, however, is not that of a "pure" dialect, as is shown by the morphological mixture: pr. 3 sg. in -*es*/-*eth*, pr. pl. in -*es*/-*eth*/-*en*/-, feminine pronoun *sche*/*he*/*a*; this scribe had trouble with the gen. pl. in -*en*, as shown by his adding *of* after *Iuen* (I 10). Not all "impure" dialects are the result of scribal interference, of course, but we seem here to have a good example of a text in one dialect copied by a scribe who imported his own usages into it. There is a strong case for assuming that the archaic and West-Midland features are original, and that the non-Western forms are scribal.

(1) Archaic features: present tenses with the *y*-prefix; frequent preservation of geminate *bb* in LIVE and HAVE; distinction between singular and plural in the past tense of some strong verbs (lost in the auxiliaries CAN and SHALL); preservation of a distinctive vowel for the pt. 2 sg. of some strong verbs; frequent use of *ac* and *myd*; occurrence of some words which have otherwise disappeared from English by this time or which did not survive past 1400.

(2) West-Midland features: feminine pronoun *a*, 2nd person plural pronoun oblique case *ou* (*ow, how*); genitive plural in -*en* (not confined to the West); superlative in -*okest*; preservation of the *i*-element in Weak Verbs of Class 2 with short root vowel; occasional *o* forms before nasals; occasional *u* for OE *y*; *ui* and *uy* spellings for OE *ȳ* and OF *ü*, spellings indicating rounding in words with OE *eo* (and also *buyrnes* for OE *beorn*); the form *botte* "bat"; perhaps the word *stuty* (if connected with early ME *stutten*).

(3) Non-Western features: plural -*es* in the words for EYE and EAR; masculine pronoun *a*; the form *pans* "pence"; occasional *a* before nasals; occasional *e* or *i*/*y* for OE *y*; *e* for OE *ēo*.

The argument that a West-Midland original was copied by a non-Western scribe (rather than the reverse) depends on internal and external factors: the persistent and deep-seated West-Midland features, especially morphological and lexical; and the strong probability that the scribe was John Wells, who almost certainly came from the East Midlands.[12] The evidence, then, points to a text copied from an exemplar that was West-Midland and linguistically old-fashioned. This is not the kind of text that would have resulted from a scribal pastiche: as a literary and linguistic forgery it would be without parallel (see above, p. 27). Even less likely is it that this linguistic patina would have been produced by someone reconstructing the text from memory. The little external evidence that we have suggests that Langland came from the West Midlands; other texts of *Piers Plowman* also contain features of English that had disapppeared from Eastern and Southern English. The linguistic appearance of **Z** suggests that it was copied from a text exactly answering to our suppositions about Langland's origins.

[12] See above, pp. 3-5.

Concordance Table

This table is designed principally to aid the reader in finding his way from one version to another, and to show the main differences in the narratives of **Z**, **A** and (less precisely) **B**; references to **C** are given only where necessary – inclusion of **C** would have made the Table very unwieldy. Brief plot synopses are provided (in the left-hand margin) simply as a guide: they do not fit the line numbers exactly. A dash (–) indicates that a line or passage is not present; a line number in parentheses means that **A** or **B** has a line corresponding to, but different from, a line in **Z**. A sequence **Z (A) (B)** means that **AB** agree against **Z**; **Z (A) B** means that **ZB** agree against **A**; **Z (A) ((B))** means that **Z**, **A** and **B** all differ; the term "exp." in the **B** column means that the **B** passage has been expanded from that in **A**. This table, however, is not designed for textual comparison: consistency in the use of brackets has not always been possible. In Passus II, to save space, comparison between **A** and **B** has been given separately in the Notes column. Differences in line-order (using **Z** as the standard) are usually shown horizontally on the line, except in the Prologue.

Section	Z	A	B	Notes
Dream begins	Pr 1-4	Pr 1-4	Pr 1-4	
	5	(K) –	–	C 1 5 ZC vs. AB
	6-16	5-15	5-15	
	17	(16)	(16)	
	18-34	17-33 — Dungeon	17-33	
Field of folk	35 Minstrels	–	–	C 1 36 ZC vs. AB
	36 "	–	–	
		(34-39) — Minstrels	(34-39)	
	37-42 Beggars	40-45	40-45	
	43-46 Friars	55-58	58-61	
	–	59-64 — More on friars	62-67	
	47-48 Hermits	50-51	53-54	
	–	52-54 — More on hermits	55-57	
	49-52 Pilgrims	46-49	46-49 + 50-52	
	53-58 Bishops etc.	96-97	217-218	
	59-60 Barons, burghers	80-82	83-85	
	61-63 Priests	(83)	(86)	
	64 "	(84-85)	(211-212)	
	65 Lawyers	86-89	213-216	
	66-69 "	90-95 — Ecclesiastics	(87-111) (expanded)	
	–		112-210 (new episode)	
	70-73 Judges	65-76	–	
	74-85 Pardoner	77-79 — Pardoner/priest	68-79	
	–		80-82	
	86-88 Tradesmen	98-100	219-221	
	89 Millers etc.	(101)	222	ZB vs. A
	90 All labourers	102-103	223	
	91-92 More labourers	104-108 — Cooks, etc.	224-225	
	–		226-230	

	Z		A		B		Notes
Holy Church teaches about	93	conclusion	109		231		
Tower, three needful	94	Transition	I (1-2)		I (1-2)		
things, warns against	95-98		3-6		3-6		
drink; Parable of coin	99-100		(7-9)		(7-9)		
due to Caesar	101-119		10-28		10-28		
	—		29		29		om. TChE
	120-129		30-39		30-41	(exp.)	
	—		40		42		om. RE
	130-144		41-55		43-57		
	145		—		—		
Holy Church teaches nature	I 1-17		I 56-72		I 58-74		
of Truth	18		—		—		
	19-22		73-76		75-78		
	23		—		—		
	24-38		77-91		79-93		
	39		—		—		
	40-64		92-116		94-127	(exp.)	
	65		—		—		
	66-84		117-132,	135, 133-134	128-144,	147, 145-146	**AB** agree on line-order
	85-99		136-150		(148-176)	(exp.)	
	100		—		—		
	101-111		151-161		177-187a		
	—		162		188		**A** I 162 = **A** I 168
	112-117		164-167,	163, 168	190-193,	189, 194	**B** I 188 = **B** I 194
	118-132		169-183		195-209		
Holy Church indicates False	II 1-3	Transition	II 1-6		II 1-6		
	4-9		—		—		
	10						

	Z	A	B	Notes
Meed's appearance	11-15	7-11	7-11	
	16	(12)	12	ZB vs. A
	17	13	13-14	
	18	14	(15-16)	B like both Z and A
			(17-18)	
Betrothal of Meed to False, planning	19-38	15-34	19-55 (exp.)	
	39	35		A 35-53 B (56-71)
	40-42	-		A 54-56 B 72-74
	43-44	36-37		A 57-66 B (75-101)
	45	Soothness		A 67-86 B 102 (103),
	46	38		104-122
	47			
	48-59	39-50		Whole passage revised
	60	(51-52)		from A to B
	61-69	53-59, 61, 60		
	70-71	-	86-87 (C III 90-91)	ZBC vs. A
	72	-		
Theology intervenes	-	62-65		
	73-93	66-86		
	94	M (86a-87)	123	ZB vs. A (except M)
	95-99	88-89, 92, 90-91	124-125, 128, 126-127	AB agree on order
	100		-	
	101-117	93-109	129-145	
	118		-	
Journey to London	119-147	110-138	146-(173)	
	148	(139)	174 ((175-177)) (178)	ZB vs. A (A 139 = B 178)
	149-159	140-150	179-189	
	160	(151)	(190)	
	161-162	152-153	191-192	
Conscience reports them	163-170	résumé	-	

Section	Z	A	B	Notes
King orders arrest	171-176	154-159	193-198	
	177	-	-	
	178-187	160-169	199-208	ZB vs. A (ZB not exact)
	188-189		209-210	
	190	(170 + 171)	(211 + 212)	
Company flees leaving Meed (+ Favel in Z)	191-213	172-194	213-235	
	214-215	(195-198)	(236-239)	
Meed at court	III 1-9	III 1-9	III 1-9	
	10	(10)	(10)	
	11-17	11-17	11-17	
	18	-	18	C IV 19
	19-31	18-30	19-31	ZBC vs. A
	32-33	WN only	-	
	34-36	31-33	32-34	C IV 33, 32
	-	(34-89) Friar, etc.	((35-100)) (exp.)	
	37-70	90-123	101-134	
	71-94	125, 124, 126-147	136, 135, 137-157	
	95	149	160	
	96	-	-	
King tries to marry Meed to Conscience	97-99	150-151, 148	161-162, 158 + (159) + (163-164)	
	100-121	152-173	165-186	
	122-124	-	-	
Conscience denounces Meed who replies	125-146	174-195	187-208	
	147-176	(196-276)	((209-353))	

(Z: Meed accuses Conscience of miserliness and says Conscience is origin of all decisions)

(A: Meed defends herself; Conscience defines two kinds of reward)

(B: expanded even further, on basis of A)

	Z	A	B	Notes
King sends for Reason	IV 1-16	IV 1-16	IV 1-16	
	17-18	17	17	
Peace complains against Wrong;	19-49 (Soothness)	18-48 EAWM only	18-19	= C v 18-19. **ZBC** vs. **A**
Meed offers compensation;	50		20-62 (exp.)	(except EAWM)
Reason refuses bail	51-118	49-116	63-133 (exp.)	
	119-121			
Reason argues with King	122-130 (**Z** V 1-9)	see below	see below	**AB** agree on order
	131	(117)	(134)	
	132			
and denounces Meed;	133-151	118-136	135-160 (exp.)	
Reason convinces court	152			
	153-156	137-140	161-164	
	157-159 King and Reason depart			**Z** conflicts with v 4
King and Reason accord;	V 1-18 (cf. IV 122-130)	IV 141-158	IV (165-170) 171-172 (173-182) 183-195	
Second Vision begins	19-33 (Wind-Word)	V 1-15	V 1-15	
	34-40			
	41-42	17-18	17-18	
	43			
	44	16	16	
	45			
Conscience (Reason) preaches	46-58	19-31	19-31	
	59-60	32-40 JEAM only	32-33	= C vi 135-136
	61-69		34-56 (exp.)	
	70			
	71-72	41-42	57-58	
	73-74			
	75	EKWM only	59	= C vi 201

	Z	A	B	Notes
Confessions: Pride, Lechery	76-90	43-57	60-74	
Envy (Wrath)	91-96 Envy, Wrath	(58-106) Envy	((75-134)) Envy	A omits Wrath
		—	(135-187) Wrath	
Covetousness	97-98 Covetousness	(107-141) Covetousness	(188-225) Covetousness	
	99-100 "	142-143 "	226-227 "	
	101	—	—	
	102-103 "	144-145 "	228-229 "	
	—	—	230-295 "	
Gluttony	104-109 Gluttony	146-206 Gluttony	(296-378) Gluttony	
		(207-212) "	(379)-384 "	
Sloth	110-129 Sloth	213-232 Sloth	(385-460) Sloth	
	130	—	—	
Robert the Robber	131-136	233-238	461-466	
	137-138	241-242	467-468	
	139-140	239-240	—	
	141	243	469	
	142-144 Wicked Steward	—	—	
	—	244	470	om. H (F)
General repentance	145-154	245-254	471-476 (= A 245-250)	
			510-512 (477-509) (= A 251-254)	
			513-524	
Pilgrimage to Truth; the pilgrim	155-166	vi 1-12		
Piers appears, gives directions to Truth:	vi 1-46	vi 13-58	v 525-571	Z 1-53: AB agree on line order
	47	66	579	
	48-49	59-60	572-573	om. MS A
	—	61	574	
Tower of Truth	50-53	62-65	575-578	
	54-65	67-78	580-591	

Description	Z		A		B	Notes
	66-67		79-80		—	
	68-72	Powers of Truth	—		—	
	73	" "	81		—	
	74-75	" "	—		—	
	76-78	Tower	—		—	
and how to enter it	79-80	Bridge, pillar	—		592-593 (+594)	= C vIII 240-241 + 242
	81-102		82-103	EAMH³ only	595-617	
	—		104-123	Seven sisters	618-642 (exp.)	
The half-acre	vII 1-30		vII 1-30		vI 1-28	
	31		—		—	
	32-47		31-46		29-51 (exp.)	
	48-49		(47-49)		(52-54)	
	50-52		50-52		55-57	
	—		53		58	
	53-54		54-55		59-60	
	55		(56)		(61)	
	56-57		57-58		62-63 (+64)	
	58		(59)		(65)	
	59		—		—	
	60		60		66	
	61		(61-69)		(67-77)	
Piers' wife, daughter	62-63		70-71	Piers' son	78-79	
Piers' son	64		(72)	" "	(80)	
	—		73-74		81-82	
	65-68	speech cont.	—		—	
	69-75	" "	75-81	speech cont.	83-89	
	76-77		(82)		(90)	
	78-90		83-95		91-103	
	91		(96)		(104)	

	Z	A	B	Notes
Ploughing the half-acre	92-106	97-111	105-119	
	107-108	–	–	
Waster, Hunger	109-169	112-172	120-184 (exp.)	
	170	–	–	
	171-195	173-197	185-211 (exp.)	
	196-201	–	–	
	202-211 *cripples*	198-207	212-221a	
	–	208-212 *needy*	222-228	
	212-229	213-230	229-246	
	230-232			
Hunger's medicine	233-237	231-234a	247-250	A 234a = B 252a (Latin)
	238	(235-236)	((251-2, 252a))	
	239-244	237-242	253-258	
	245	–	–	
	246-259	243-256 *physicians*	259-272	
	260-278 *physicians*	(257-258)	(273-274)	
Hunger demands dinner	279-285	259-265	275-281	Reduced to two lines AB
	286	(266)	(282)	
	287-315	267-295	283-311	
	316	–	–	
	317-328	296-307	312-326 (exp.)	
	–	–	327-331 prophecy	
			–	
Pardon from Truth	VIII 1-68	VIII 1-67	VII 1-65	
	69	–	–	
	70-74	68-72	66-90 (exp.)	
	75-76	–	–	
	77-88	73-84	91-102	
	89-90	(85-86)	(103-104)	

	Z	A	B	Notes
	91-92	87-88	105-106	
Intrusion of Priest	Q¹ 93-95	89-91	107-109	
	–	92	110	
	96	(95-96)	(113-114)	Q misplaces Latin
	97-98	93-94	111-112	
	99-110	97-109	115-127	
	111-112	110a-110	128a-128	;
	113-126	111-124	129-142	
	127-128	125a-125	143a-143	;
Dreamer awakes and muses	129-189	126-184	144-206	;
	190-191 couplet	–	–	;

C1